MW01517968

INVESTING IN FILMS
The 12.5 Secrets
Elite Investors Keep for
Themselves

A Survival Kit
for High Net Worth Individuals
and Hedge Funds
Looking for Sound Investments
in Independent Film

By
René Bourdages

Beverly Hills, CA

Printed and bounded in the United States of America
Published by ELEVADO MEDIA, Inc.
433 N Camden Dr, 6th floor
Beverly Hills, CA 90210

Disclaimer
Every reasonable effort has been made to ensure the accuracy of the
information contained in *INVESTING IN FILMS: The 12.5 Secrets
Elite Investors Keep for Themselves*. ELEVADO MEDIA, Inc. cannot
be held responsible for any inaccuracies, or the misrepresentation of
those mentioned in the book.

Print ISBN 9780692283011

This book is dedicated to my parents, Jeannine and Maurice Bourdages who taught me the value of hard work, integrity, love and courage.

Disclaimer

This book is designed to help readers understand business issues frequently encountered in the filmed entertainment industry. It will provide you with an understanding of basic business principles, enabling you to better communicate with your business partners and advisors.

The information contained in this book is intended to provide general information and does not constitute financial or legal advice. This book is not intended to create a consultant-client relationship between you and the author or any of his associates, and you should not act or rely on any information in this book without seeking the advice of an attorney and an experienced media & entertainment advisor.

The information provided is not a substitute for consulting with an experienced attorney and receiving counsel based on the facts and circumstances of a particular transaction. Many of the business and legal principles mentioned herein are subject to exceptions and qualifications that may not be noted in the text. Furthermore, case law and statutes are subject to revision and may not apply in every state or country. Because of the quick pace of technological change, some of the information in this book may be outdated by the time you read it. Readers should be aware that business practices, distribution methods, and legislation continue to evolve in the rapidly changing entertainment industries.

PARTICULAR PURPOSE, REGARDING THE INFORMATION. THE AUTHOR DOES NOT GUARANTEE THE COMPLETENESS, ACCURACY, OR TIMELINESS OF THIS INFORMATION. YOUR USE OF THIS INFORMATION IS AT YOUR OWN RISK

Rene Bourdages can be contacted by email. However, if you communicate with him electronically or otherwise in connection with a matter for which he does not already represent you, your communication may not be treated as privileged or confidential. A consultant-client relationship can only be created with a written retainer agreement signed by both parties.

Acknowledgements

This book was made possible through the support of many friends and industry experts and I want to acknowledge their support, their inspiration and their precious input:

Ken Markman, Bill Grantham, late Tom Sherak, Clark Peterson, Maxime Rémillard, Danté Marshall, Richard Kiratsoulis, Rob Aft, Ellen Pittleman, Randy Greenberg, Marc Lapointe, Mark Kudlow, Marie-Aude Pigeon, Scott Allan Morgan, Jean de Meuron, Denyse Gagnon, Lisa de Wilde, Max Desmarais, David Carter, Peter Graham, Herman Weigel, Micah Green, Jeremy Spry, Odile Méthot, André Bureau, late Harold Greenberg, Ian Greenberg, Stephen Greenberg, Jean Bureau, Patrice Théroux, Henri-Paul Rousseau, Michel Houle, Richard Goudreault, Michel Pradier, Joëlle Levie, François Macerola, Stéphane Giguère, Michel Tremblay and Bill Atkinson.

« An investment in knowledge pays the best interest. »

Benjamin Franklin

Contents

Happiness is not in the mere possession of money; it lies in the joy of achievement, in the thrill of creative effort. –

Franklin D. Roosevelt

Why Investors Should Read this Book

Yield has become increasingly harder to find

In a world where interest rates have become persistently anemic, where the bond market has morphed into a massive and depressing refuge for investors disenchanted with stocks and real estate, there is real pressure on hedge and pension funds, family offices and wealth management companies to generate higher yields.

Film investment represents a sound alternative investment in a portfolio

The Great recession of 2008 has reminded us that stocks, bonds and real estate are not immune to market fluctuations. Finding alternative investment strategies has become a priority for many elite investors. Filmed entertainment, to a large degree, has proven to be an excellent buffer against those fluctuations, achieving record years for worldwide box-office receipts - every year since 2008.

Panoramic thinking and Risk-tolerance have become essential survival tools.

Alternative investments experts such as Bob Rice[1], believe that investment portfolios should be both "panoramic" and "risk-tolerant". By panoramic, we mean a true diversity of asset classes and strategies for both income and growth over a relatively sustainable period of time. Whereas risk tolerance, for its part, implies active risk management over a relatively long period of time – one of the main focuses of this book – while the investments themselves should provide returns uncorrelated to

---

[1] The Alternative Answer, The Nontraditional Investments that Drive the World's Best-Performing Portfolios, Bob Rice

fluctuations in the economy and vulnerability levels that are also diversified.

Risk is part of business. Manage it.

In my experience - I have spoken to hundreds of savvy entrepreneurs in my career – investors know that risk is an integral part of any business. Smart investors want to be able to identify potential risks and find ways to mitigate them to the best of their knowledge in order to turn these same risks into rewards.

Don't trip on that red carpet!

If all industries carry a certain degree of business risk, most don't benefit from the appealing nature of filmed entertainment, which has the power to attract a lot of people. When the level of risk between two types of investment is comparable – say a real estate project and a film financing project – many ultra high net worth individuals go for the film project as it carries a definite level of glamour and hype that's hard to match in other industries.

Being invited to the film set during shooting and attending the world premiere of a film that you helped financed - and for which you receive an executive producer credit – are nice perks. In the same vein, walking the red carpet in Cannes or Los Angeles is something not all wealthy individuals can brag about - and we don't blame film investors for enjoying it.

But as one can surely appreciate the stardom surrounding that industry, a consultant's job is to make sure that there are no hidden bumps that might trip investors – reducing risk and maximizing ROI. An investor's ongoing trust is a consultant's biggest asset.

Creating Alpha in film investments

Investment managers assess mutual fund performances by tracking the "alpha", the difference between the return advertised by funds and the industry benchmark. If the concept of creating alpha were to be also applied to filmed entertainment, this book - and the sum of its recommendations, which are based on years of research and years of experience - would provide you with the tools to significantly improve your alpha.

A book for investors

During my thirty-four year career in media and entertainment, I have helped create original content and have acquired motion pictures, TV series and high-profile sporting events for private companies, wealthy individuals and investment funds. And during that time, I've had my share of both stellar successes and humbling disappointments.

Back in 2002, I also had the opportunity to be one of the very first to negotiate 360-degree rights deals on media properties with some of the largest media companies in the world.

As I continue my professional journey in this fascinating industry, I've become more and more aware of – and concerned by - stories about film investors entering into one-sided business agreements, being improperly advised. I believe that had they known what to ask for, and what to look for, they would have made much more favorable deals. If this industry can indeed be called a jungle fraught with danger, then investors need an experienced professional guide to help them effectively navigate around these dangers.

This was the driver to launch my own consulting practice, ELEVADO Media in Beverly Hills, CA; to provide independent advisory to professionals navigating the media and entertainment industry. I've surrounded myself with very smart people who constantly raise the bar while sharing my commitment to excellence and common sense. Our cumulative experience is impressive - but as we get older, we prefer not to add it all up.

And with all that experience, I've decided that it was high time that I write the first book about how investors can cautiously deploy capital in film financing transactions while adding alpha without excessive risk. And here it is.

A fast read

This book has intentionally been crafted to be a quick read for busy business professionals. It focuses on what the best investors have been secretly doing in recent times. Most people have read the 12.5 chapters in less than two hours. It's shorter than a movie and perfect for that train or airplane commute.

Boiling it down to one paragraph...

If you want to diversify your portfolio with an asset class that is isolated from most systemic risks, investing in filmed entertainment, all things considered, may be very compelling. With proper guidance, the inherent risk can be significantly reduced and the return optimized to a degree where you can potentially outperform the typical performance of the sector and have fun doing it.

So fasten your seatbelts and hold on to your hat... and your calculator, and enjoy the ride!

"I never attempt to make money on the stock market. I buy on the assumption that they could close the market the next day and not reopen it for ten years."

–Warren Buffett

INTRODUCTION

From cave walls to the big screen, storytelling is here to stay

At the dawn of humankind, men used the inside walls of their cave to tell extraordinary tales about the fascinating world outside. We can imagine that fiction was a big part of the story as their imagination fueled the narrative. But if storytelling today is still a very creative art, it has reached such a level of refinement, sophistication and technical achievement that it sometimes feels more real than reality itself. Think of CGI (Computer Generated Imagery) live action films such as Gravity playing on an IMAX 3D screen that fills 10,000 sq. ft. Indeed, very few modes of telling stories are as complex (and resource-intensive) as cinematography.

Filmmaking is a unique collaborative process that requires vast human, technical and financial resources to be harnessed in a rigorous, creative process. Because of that unique process, investing in film necessitates certain conditions and guidelines to make sure that investors are protected and the film is successful with audiences. In other words, the business aspect of filmmaking has become so important these days that I felt investors should have the opportunity to learn about best practices to improve their chances of a favorable ROI.

This book is designed for investors who want to better understand the fascinating world of independent film financing. Over the last decades, independent films have grown in number, genre and size and are credited for bringing an incredible array of stories to worldwide audiences, complementing the movies made by the Hollywood studios. Likewise, the financial tools available have also evolved dramatically over time.

I've read dozens of books on independent film production and film financing but I could not find one that was specifically written for film investors or, as we call them in the film industry, "film financiers". This is not a book about studio films, or how to invest in studios or distribution companies. To be absolutely clear, this book aims to help investors find the best business opportunities in selective independent highly commercial feature films for the international and domestic markets.

There's a big difference between "independent films" and "art-house" indie films. They're both produced and financed outside of the studio system, but art-house films typically have limited theatrical distribution and are screened mostly at film festivals, where they sometimes win awards and benefit from free publicity. They often appeal to smaller niche audiences of cinephiles, which limits the number of distributors who will risk taking on the marketing and distribution costs of these films. For a financier, they are often a philanthropy vehicle and cannot provide a solid financial ROI.

Investors looking for decent ROI are usually leaning towards independent films whose stories have wide appeal, recognizable talent and high marketability that allow for a theatrical release. This very type of film is the focus of this book, which will reveal what these independent film investors are doing to mitigate the various risks and to optimize their returns. In the title of this book, I call them "secrets," but there is no magic to it. In fact, these investors follow a simple common sense approach and stick to practices that are always logical.

Many of these financiers keep their practices to themselves, thinking it gives them a competitive edge, but I caution against this. If more investors were knowledgeable about the do's and don'ts of film financing - of the pitfalls and the traps as well as the available risk mitigation tools that should be in place - they would get a better experience from the process and our industry would only be the better for it.

By the time you finish this short book, I hope you'll gain more insight on how to invest in film and how to help bring great stories to the world, from script to screen, while earning a favorable ROI.

Oh, and as many people have wondered, **why 12.5 secrets?** This is just my way to keep in mind that the smallest details such as half an interest point can make a big difference between loss and profit when it comes to filmmaking. Never overlook the little details...

"Money often costs too much."

–Ralph Waldo Emerson

Chapter 1:
Most Films Don't Make a Profit. Understand Why!

Most films don't make a net profit!

Only a small percentage of the films produced make a net profit, yet people continue to invest in them... This is probably the most surprising news to any potential investor in the film and entertainment industry. Even today, much mystery surrounds how revenues and expenses flow in and out of a film project.

The process of producing a feature film is capital-intensive and most of the costs are committed before the product is released to an audience. The commercial success is very hard to predict despite extensive research. Here is why so many films don't make a profit.

For starters, many of the films produced never find distribution, which is absolutely essential to generate revenues. Of the 4,000 or so films submitted to Sundance on a given year, only 120 will be selected and a mere dozen will be acquired by a distributor for more than 1 million dollars. In fact, fewer than 700 films are released each year in the United States. The vast majority of the features produced will never find a distributor.

Secondly, many films picked up by distributors will never get a theatrical release. The distributor will not always be able to book theater screens with exhibitors and to find the dollars for Prints & Advertising (commonly called P&A) to distribute physical or virtual prints of the film and to advertise the release in major media outlets. A theatrical release is still a crucial exhibition window for building awareness and profile for the film in subsequent windows. It often sets the sales price in other platforms of exhibition such as Pay TV and Free TV. More importantly, an independent film that has secured domestic (US and Canada) theatrical distribution will have a better chance of triggering other sources of revenues, such as pre-licensing of international territories and ancillary sales.

Thirdly, even when a film is picked up for distribution and gets a theatrical release, different stakeholders, such as sales agents, senior lenders, mezzanine lenders, gap financiers, bond companies, distributors, executive producers, talent, and so on, will collect some type of fee in many of the various windows of exhibition, reducing the probability of an actual breakeven and delaying that breakeven point over time. It creates a situation where most stakeholders in the project prefer to grab a fee upfront, rather than wait for a net profit. So technically, the film can make some money or even a lot of money but often little or no net profit.

Never forget the exhibitors
I'm still puzzled that most entertainment trade publications provide domestic and worldwide box office earnings alongside the film's production budget. It gives readers the impression that a film that generates $100 million at the box office on a production budget of $50 million has exceeded the breakeven point and thus turned in a profit. That is simply incorrect.

The exhibitor's share
Trades omit what industry insiders know too well: that cinema exhibitors keep approximately 50% of the gross box office receipts. The share payable to exhibitors is based on complex formulas negotiated with each distributor that change on a weekly basis, but as a rule of thumb, about half of the box office revenues stays with the theaters. In addition, the exhibitor will also get concession revenues, but will have to pay for the theater's expenses. In some instances,

the parties will negotiate a fixed weekly amount as a floor for the theater. This weekly amount is called the "house nut". If ticket sales are low, the first dollars in revenue will go to cover the theater's house nut until fully paid, the balance being shared between the theater owner and the distributor in accordance with the predetermined split.

The distributor's share

The remaining 50% then goes to the distributor and is referred to as "theatrical rentals". Immediately, the distribution company (whether one of the major studios or an independent distributor) will keep a distribution fee of anywhere between 20-35% of those theatrical rentals.

The Prints & Advertising Costs (P&A)

The next costs to be repaid from the first dollars are usually the P&A, which includes the costs of advertising for the release of the film and the various copies of the film (prints) made for the exhibitors. This cost is NEVER included in the film's budget. And without P&A money, forget about significant theatrical distribution. Many films never secure P&A and hence experience a very limited release, which is never a good story for investors.

The producer and the equity investors will usually start receiving some money to offset the production costs only after the distribution fee and the P&A loans are recouped. And, as we will see in later chapters, other stakeholders may extract fees before the equity investor and the producer can get a piece of the back-end.

As we can see in Table 1 below, a feature film with a budget of $50 million that generates a domestic box office of $100 million will not be able to repay its production costs solely from the theatrical exploitation of the film. The payment of a distribution fee and the repayment of the $35 million P&A spending will only leave a surplus of $2.5 million to go against the cost of production. The loss after theatrical will be a staggering $47.5 million.

Table 1 Typical domestic revenue flow from an independent film

Assumptions				
Domestic box office		$100,000,000		
Negative Cost (Production Budget)		$50,000,000		
P&A Budget		$35,000,000		
		Revenue	**Expenses**	**Total**
Domestic theatrical				
Domestic box office		$100,000,000		
Less Domestic exhibitors share	50%		($50,000,000)	
Domestic Theatrical Rentals				$50,000,000
Less distribution fee	25%		($12,500,000)	
				$37,500,000
Less repayment of P&A			($35,000,000)	
Net proceeds after theatrical window				$2,500,000
Less Negative cost *(production cost)*			($50,000,000)	
Net Profit (loss) after negative cost				**($47,500,000)**

The importance of international sales and ancillary sales

In some instances, a film may reach the breakeven point with international sales and ancillary sales.

International sales are often achieved through a sales agent who's role is basically to sell the project to different distributors in various international territories and seek firm commitments in the form of pre-licensing agreements (commonly called presales).

Ancillary rights consist of non-theatrical revenues like prisons, hotels, military bases, home video revenues, pay per view revenues, subscription, video-on-demand (VOD), pay TV (HBO, Showtime, Cinemax, etc.) as well as cable and free TV revenues. However, it is important to note that in each of these windows of exploitation, a distribution fee and various expenses will be deducted from the gross revenues generated by the film therein before any money flows back to the producer and his investors.

Time is money

As smart investors know too well, a return on investment (ROI) is always affected by the recoupment timeline, therefore, the more successive windows you need to break even, the longer the capital is at risk and at work.

In the filmed entertainment industry, you are often presented with projections that provide, say, a 15% return on investment. But if you disburse your capital early, as an equity investor, and the film takes 4-5 years to make it to the screen, your annual ROI will be a fraction of that.

Seasoned film investors always ask for a recoupment timeline backed up by a thorough revenue projection for each revenue stream. This book will give you more details about the typical revenue waterfall and its importance in terms of negotiations.

A good story is the foundation

Remember that a film's success always starts with a great story well told (to which I'll dedicate an entire chapter). People's tastes are becoming increasingly complex and eclectic. But fragmented audiences are nonetheless looking for unifying experiences[2], and a great screenplay with the right director and talented actors has more chances to fill that need. Every year we see many films have a memorable impact on large audiences. It happens all the time.

Unfortunately, many films released are based around an average screenplay, and in today's day and age, average is mediocre and therefore unacceptable.

Even if you were to attach the best actors - the brightest stars with a strong social media following - a

---

[2] This quote is attributed to Ken Markman, UCLA Extension instructor in his class Marketing Entertainment: Strategies for the Global Market.

mediocre screenplay will sabotage the entire project. If you believe that putting more capital, acting talent and marketing dollars behind a project will offset a bad screenplay, you are heading for disaster.

Open on Friday... or die.

Choosing a film on a Friday night is a decision affected by many last minute variables. Depending on whom you are with, the genre of films you pick will vary. If you prefer a theater closer to work and the screening time is too tight, you may revert to another film choice or simply skip the movie altogether and go for drinks. Weather can play a significant role; a snowstorm on the East Cost of the United States will severely impact the box-office. Conversely, a heat wave may fill the theaters with people looking for a refreshing escape. Most importantly, the other new releases for the same weekend are extremely important.

Complementary releases are always better

An independent film has more chances of success if it is complementary to a blockbuster release. On may 4th 2012, *Marvel's The Avengers* opened on 4,349 screens with the highest grossing weekend of all times: $207 million. The very same weekend, Fox Searchlight had the brilliance to release the $10 million indie film *The Best Exotic Marigold Hotel* on 27 screens as a platform release. The performance per screen was so impressive that it eventually secured 1,300 screens and generated $46 million domestically and close to $137 million worldwide! From an investor perspective, this is a stellar performance.

In a nutshell

As an investor, you absolutely need to understand how much revenue is realistically and conservatively expected from the theatrical release, and also from the following windows of exploitation.

But most importantly, you want to understand who will be entitled to fees, residuals, off the tops, gross points, etc., before some money flows back to the producer and/or yourself. This is called the "waterfall" or the recoupment schedule[3]. By understanding the intricacies of the interparty agreement that ultimately dictates how the recoupment will happen, and in which order, you will be more knowledgeable than many investors that have financed films in the past. You would be amazed to see how financiers often fail to ask questions, and end up being taken for a ride.

Equity Investors Beware

At the present time, according to the Hollywood Reporter, Universal is in a legal battle with Elliot Management, a hedge fund from New York, that claims it is the victim of fraudulent accounting. History seems to repeat itself: in 2011, Paramount settled a lawsuit from Melrose Investors 2 LP [4], which complained that it hadn't seen a dollar of profit after making a $375 million investment in 2006 for 29 studio films that garnered gross cumulative revenues of $7 billion.

To me, the underlying message here is that even when films make money, if you don't fully understand, and thoroughly negotiate, how and when you will be able to recoup your investment, you may never see a penny because so many parties will have access to the revenue stream before you can get your principal and your premium back.

Net Points = Monkey Points[5]

Because very few films will turn a net profit, net points (or percentage points of net profits) are worth almost nothing and the seasoned stakeholders try to recoup money on gross performance as high as possible in the food chain.

---

3 The waterfall recoupment is also referred sometimes as the "capital stack". However, some parties to recoupment of revenues have not invested in capital necessarily.
4 Paramount Pictures Corp. on January 11, 2013 resolved a $375 million fraud suit by Melrose Investors 2 LP which claimed it had helped finance more than two dozen films but had not received any profits.
5 The term "Monkey Points" was coined by the actor Eddie Murphy. He also said "only a fool would accept net points in their contract". He always insisted on gross points.

Financiers and their advisors have a responsibility to understand who gets paid before them, and because contracts are always lengthy, complex and convoluted, they should always ask the producer and the distributor to explain how precisely the money flows back. Who exactly gets what before us? You will be surprised by the answer, or lack thereof. Don't be afraid to ask why. As an investor, at the due diligence stage, you have leverage; your capital will be at risk and your priority position in the waterfall should be in accordance.

Hollywood and the never-ending search for capital

Since their creation more than a century ago, Hollywood studios have always attracted the attention of wealthy individuals. Because of the aura of glamour, celebrity, fame, and talent, it's always been a "sexy" industry, and studio executives as well as film producers have exploited that sexiness wholeheartedly by raising significant amounts of capital from hedge funds, private equity funds, pensions funds, Wall Street firms and high net worth individuals.

Investors have become increasingly smarter

With time, investors have become more knowledgeable. Money is smarter now. Media and business newspapers have published several stories of investors, both individual and institutional, that came to Hollywood looking for fame and fortune and lost their entire investments only to return silently to where they came from. These stories have been amplified by legal actions as well. Conversely, profitable investors are more discreet and often keep a low profile in an industry known for its egotistic executives.

Despite the downfall of some investors, the film industry is still a vibrant, recession-proof industry that provides returns usually uncorrelated to the current state of the economy.

The movie studios system

The studios, also called the majors, are essentially large distribution entities with production facilities such as sound stages and back lots. They are Disney, Warner, Paramount, Universal, Sony and MGM. New distributors, such as Lionsgate and The Weinstein Company, have a quasi studio status although they don't own back lots.

In recent years, Studios have been focusing more and more on producing and releasing a limited number of franchise-able, hundred million plus tent pole properties, such as super hero sequels, prequels and stories from best-selling books all over the world. They allocate more of their production funds and capital to fewer films per year, and mitigate their risk by concentrating on properties already known to the public. But the fact is studios make the bulk of their profit from distribution. This is where the money is the most easily recoupable as we saw in Table 1. Their current focus on bigger budget films has created a need for studios to pick-up independent films to complement their distribution slate.

The independent film

By definition, an independent film is one that is produced and financed outside of the studio system. An independent film can be distributed by a major studio or one of its indie divisions and still be considered independent. Studios will charge various fees to producers in exchange for access to their sophisticated distribution infrastructure.

The studios themselves are always looking for new capital, preferably from equity investors with whom they can share the risk of releasing all of these films. I'm always curious to understand why studios are constantly looking for new equity money. If a studio's existing equity partners were satisfied with the returns provided, why wouldn't they reinvest with that same studio? The studio wouldn't have to look for new capital all the time...

Chapter 1 Conclusion

- Many films never make a profit because many stakeholders are entitled to receive fees before a movie can reach the breakeven point.
- Many films never secure proper distribution. The ones who do often don't recoup all their costs because of the additional expense of commercially releasing a film on a large scale.
- Theaters usually keep about half of the box office and send the other half to the film's distributor.
- Prints & Advertising spending and distribution fees are deducted in priority from the first dollar received by distributor, before anyone else gets repaid.
- Equity investors in films are generally the last to see a return on their investment.
- The players who take a fee before profit are usually in a better position.
- The Hollywood studios now focus on a smaller number of big-budget homemade productions each year. They prefer high concept films that already enjoy some degree of public awareness and are part of a promising franchise.
- Successful independent filmmakers can secure distribution from studios or independent distributors.

"Buy when everyone else is selling and hold until everyone else is buying. That's not just a catchy slogan. It's the very essence of successful investing."

–J. Paul Getty

Chapter 2:
Some Film Investors Are Very Successful:
They Are Selective!

If so many films don't make a net profit, how can there be successful film investors in the entertainment space? What are their secrets? What techniques are they using?

Achieving balance between story, audience and profit.
First of all, they always take a close look at the first element; what is the story, and is it worth telling it? Secondly, what's the real audience for this story? And finally, at what cost can it be made to reach that audience and be profitable?

These are the first fundamental questions that successful investors are looking at. We'll have a chance to detail these elements in Chapter 8.

Spreading the risk and the upside.
Smart investors don't put all their eggs in one basket. Instead, they are selective and diversify their investments across a couple of projects. They stay away from investing in a what I call a "blind" slate of films for which an investor has no say in what film is being financed. Such an investment does not provide enough visibility into the value of each project unless a form of solid collateral such as a letter of credit mitigates your risk.

Being selective is paramount. It means having to choose and having to often say no. The ability to say no, to pass on a project, is indispensable.

Asking why

An experienced financier will first ask that one simple question of any filmmaker looking for an investment: "Why do you want to make this film?" You would be surprised how many producers will be caught off guard, but the answer to this question is crucial. It will provide insight on the driving forces behind the project and should strike a chord with the investor because his capital will be entrusted with this producer to deliver the final product based on that very vision.

Look at soft monies

Smart film investors maximize tax credits and soft monies to offset their risks. In the United States alone, there are 43 states that offer some form of tax incentives for film production. Other countries also provide competitive tax credits to attract film productions. In fact, the concept of film production incentives started in Canada and expanded to many other countries. Smart investors will look at the best way to tell that story in the best location for the best cost.

Your life should not depend on a film investment

Film investors should never invest more than they can afford to lose. Keep in mind that this is a risky business and that's why they should be able to afford losing that money, as they focus first and foremost on capital preservation.

Don't "fall in love"

Smart film investors are not star-struck. In a recent industry Conference, indie film financier Michael Benaroya, when asked how he goes about investing in a project, stated that at the negotiation stage and the development stage, he tries to distance himself from the creative people because he wants to maintain his independent judgment and not "fall in love" with the director or the project at the expense of his rational decision making.

Not all types of investments are worth the same

Experienced financiers usually look at more than just the pure equity investment opportunity. They often act as senior lenders or subordinated lenders, or as we call it mezzanine or gap lenders. They can also lend money to the production for a P&A budget, and sometimes include the acquisition of specific territories along with their investment. Some of these options may be available at the early stages of negotiation, if the investor understands the full concept of the financial structure, and if he, or his advisor, has a relationship with the other partners, whether they are banks, foreign sales agencies, distributors or completion guarantors, etc.

The budget needs to be right

Savvy investors take a serious look at all budget costs with an eye on lowering the risk without affecting the production value. Every dollar unnecessarily spent on the film takes it a dollar further away from breaking even. All costs should be optimized, vendors negotiated and locations compared so that the budget continues to make sense in the context of its target audience and revenue forecasts. Before a financier asks, say, to reduce the number of shooting days, or reduce the budget on special effects, he should always be careful of what that target audience will be looking for in the film. There are probably other costs in the budget that would have less impact on the production value and these should be scrutinized beforehand. Prudent cost reduction of some budget elements can make a big difference in terms of profit or loss at the end.

Bonds, chain of title and essential elements

Wise investors will ask questions about how money will flow in and out. As an investor, don't be afraid to ask if you think that a definition or formula is blurry; simply say "give me a concrete example of how this will work" and if the answer is not reflective of the agreement, simply ask for the agreement to better reflect the answer.

A good investor should require a completion guarantee (often termed as a "bond") where a third party, the bond company, will guarantee that the film will be completed on time, on budget, and delivered to the distributor. This is crucial. If you put your money in a film that is not bonded, you may well end up losing all your investment with no significant recourse. If the production stops, and the film is not bonded, you may lose the totality of your investment. The circumstances that can end or severely impact a production or a numerous and diversified: injury and extreme weather (Terry Gilliam's ill-fated "The Man Who Killed Don Quixote"), death of the lead actor ("Dark Blood", starring the regretted River Phoenix), financial troubles (Orson Welles' never completed "The Other Side of the Wind") or simply "Star problems" (George Cukor's "Something's Got To Give", which was to star Marilyn Monroe).

Successful investors ask a lawyer to provide an opinion on the validity of the chain of title. The chain of title traces the route by which the producer acquired the right to use copyrighted material from the author through a "chain" of assignments and transfers. It is the foundation of the asset. It's what guarantees that you have a clearly defined underlying property on which you're building a film.

Seasoned film financiers will also make sure that all "essential elements" of the film, namely, primary cast and crew, are insured. Otherwise, in the event one of the lead actors becomes unable to fulfill his obligations or, God forbid, be injured or die during production, the investors' capital would not be protected.

Understand the source of revenue and the quality of projections

Successful film investors always have a precise idea of who gets repaid before them, and what their real inherent risk is. They will look at how they can potentially be repaid, how the projected revenue flow will help them recoup their principal and then their premium. Some film investors will be recouping from international sales revenue. In that case, they will only accept foreign sales estimates that are originating from a handful of recognized foreign sales agents; the ones against which the bank is willing to advance money should be the ones from which you take advice. It's always preferable to have a third party assessment or a third party opinion about the sales estimates provided.

Know the people who recoup before you

If the film investor is a subordinate lender, in the sense that there is a senior lender in first priority before him, that investor (if he's cautious) will understand the degree of risk the bank is taking. A bank in a senior position that takes too much of a risk makes the deal for the subordinate lender less desirable. Always understand the deal ahead of you and how it can impact your own deal.

Know your producer

Elite film investors do their homework by thoroughly assessing the producer's track record, his reputation and his ability to deliver the project before him. Common sense dictates that the producer's personality will impact the whole project, as the producer is ultimately in charge of all of the films deliverables. His leadership style, his rigor, and his ethics will cascade into all of the crewmembers involved in the production of the film. If you're not comfortable with the producer, run in the opposite direction! The producer's ability to deliver a good product represents a major element of the execution risk.

Delineate legal issues and business issues.

Many investors will not let their lawyer make business decisions on their behalf. Dealing business points is singularly different from negotiating legal clauses. In addition, business risks are sometimes quite different from legal risks, and during a due diligence process, both types of risk should be well laid out and addressed. Ultimately the business decision made by the investor should be based on separate assessments of both legal and business/execution risks and how both types of risks can be successfully mitigated.

Who's really an A-list actor these days?

Investors should not be fooled by so-called producers who claim they have "A-list" actors/directors without naming them. Such claims do not equate to confirmed commitments. If they did indeed have the talent attached, they would mention their names. And surprisingly, very few well-known actors are A-list stars[6] considered "bankable", that is, able to generate pre-licensed contracts in foreign territories based solely on their involvement in a project.

Show your capital early and negotiate thoroughly

Successful film investors are opportunistic. They show the availability of their funds quickly to speak from a position of strength to the production company looking for capital. Negotiation is often about leverage.

However, they will hold on disbursing any of these funds until a proper escrow disbursement agreement has been negotiated and executed. Such an agreement will include many important preceding conditions and a disbursement mechanism that will allow for a proper due diligence before any capital is deployed. They assess everything seriously before the film financing closes.

Track costs

Once their capital is invested in a given film, smart investors keep an eye on costs throughout principal photography and post-production, so that expenses are kept under control and contingencies remain unspent unless absolutely necessary. We've seen examples where an unspent 10% contingency reserve was used to accelerate the reimbursement of the senior debt, so that other equity partners and investors in the film could benefit from a faster recoupment.

---

[6] The A+ Star rating and the overall concept of a Hot list of actors has been developed into a form of science by James Ulmer.

Only a fraction of investors keep a close eye on those weekly cost reports because many people believe that the assigned bond company is responsible for tracking costs as part of their mandate. This is partly true. Bond companies know that there is a 10% contingency already built into the budget, so they don't have to extend their own money before that money is used. For that reason, investors and financiers of the film are the ones who should be closely tracking these unspent contingencies to make sure that any savings can be preserved and eventually used to lower their financial risk.

Look at other deals that could impact you

As an equity investor, successful financiers are sensitive to the negotiations between the producer and the distributor; in particular, they look at what fees are negotiated and, how profit participation is defined; there are so many ways to define profit participation, sometimes these definitions can consume 25 pages of a single contract.

Smart investors also take a serious look at the domestic distribution agreement between the producer and the distributor. I will cover many of the key issues related to distribution in Chapter 9.

Chapter 2 Conclusion

- Start with a good story.
- Assess the audience potential and the revenue potential to determine the optimal budget required to successfully reach that audience and expect a reasonable profit.
- Gradually diversify your investments in various projects, ideally into different genres aiming at different market segments.
- Ask questions.
- Leverage tax incentives.

- Assess the ability of the producer to deliver an excellent project on time and on budget.
- Segregate legal and business points; address each one to your satisfaction.
- Show your funds swiftly but; disburse cautiously, ideally through an escrow agreement.
- Tracks costs thoroughly.
- Understand and negotiate your position in the waterfall recoupment.

"Opportunity is missed by most people because it is dressed in overalls and looks like work."

–Thomas Edison

Chapter 3
Opportunities Are Growing

An industry in growth mode, uncorrelated to the economy

Despite the fact that the press routinely predicts the decline of the movie industry, it is in fact growing. According to the Motion Picture Association of America, global box office receipts for all films released around the world increased by 4% from the previous year, reaching $35.9 billion in 2013.

Table 2   Global box office – All films (US$ billions)
Source MPAA 2013

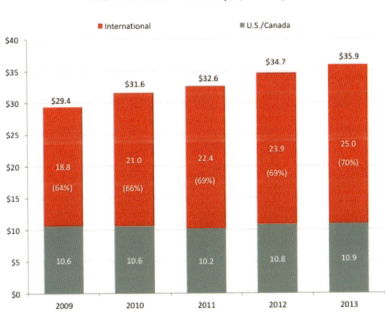

Global Box Office – All Films (US$ Billions)

The U.S./Canada box office was up 1% over last year to $10.9 billion despite a decline in admissions in 2013, due to an increase in average ticket price (+2%).

Movies are recession-proof

The box office has historically been uncorrelated to Wall Street and the economy at large. Even in 2009, in the darkest moments of the Great Recession, the US & Canada box office established a new record high at $10.6 billion. For many investors, film has become an attractive alternative to more traditional investments. Indeed, for these investors looking to balance their portfolio with an asset class that does not hinge on the vicissitudes of Wall Street, this holds obvious appeal. The entertainment industry has been historically less affected by economic cycles because even today, a movie still offers one of the most affordable entertainment options, costing less than 40 dollars for a family outing of four.

Table 3. Average Ticket Price for a Family of Four (US$)
Source: MPAA 2013

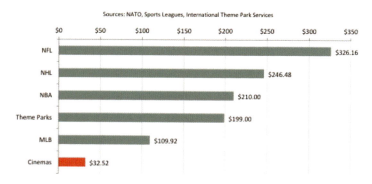

The growth is increasingly international

It is clear, however, that international markets are fueling the growth for films. There are many emerging markets that are building more and more screens, giving access to new audiences, for studio movies and independent films. Markets like Russia, Brazil and, China, the burgeoning BRIC countries, grew 36% in 2012. Hence, international sales agents have an ever-increasing influence in terms of what films get green lit, and international co-productions can also facilitate the financing and the performance in a given market.

China: the next Hollywood frontier... but how?

The Chinese market has been increasing dramatically. Box office in China has grown by 27 percent in 2013, to reach a stunning $3.6 billion, becoming the first international market to exceed $3 billion. However, there are currently issues with Chinese government censorship of films that mandate the use of caution when evaluating film revenue projections for the Chinese market. Film investors can potentially end up in a situation where their film can be denied access to the Chinese market for censorship reasons, thus jeopardizing their chances of recouping their investment and that could create a risk for the investors trying to recoup out of Chinese presales. For instance, Quentin Tarantino's Academy Award winner *Django Unchained* was interrupted just a few minutes into its premiere screening in China, whereas and *Noah*, starring Russell Crowe, was denied entry into China for obscure reasons. The list of films that never made into the Chinese market is almost as long as the Great Wall of China... Additionally, in recent years, some of the Hollywood studios were still struggling to secure blockbuster revenues stemming from the Chinese territory. Hence, even though emerging markets offer great opportunities, they also involve certain risks.

The digital conversion continues

As of 2013, 80 percent of the world's nearly 135,000 cinema screens had switched to digital. (See table 4)

Table 4 2013 Cinema Screens by Format and Region
Source: MPAA Theatrical Stats 2013

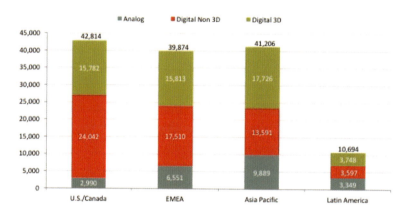

Although digitization of film processing and duplication is cheaper, distributors are currently subsidizing the conversion of theaters screens by allocating a virtual print fee to exhibitors in exchange for their ongoing conversion to digital projectors. The benefit for the distributor and its exhibitor is to react more quickly to audience preference by not requiring a single print for each projection room. Switching projection rooms in a Cineplex based on demand is therefore much easier.

For production companies, the digital support brings more flexibility, in particular for smaller budgets films. Conversely, CGI effects are growing in popularity and marketing costs are still soaring. So despite the digital conversion, no significant economies have materialized yet for the industry.

On the home media front, the rapid decline of physical sales of DVD has not yet been totally offset by the increasing digital VOD and streaming revenues.

Fewer studio films; more independent films
As I mentioned before, Hollywood studios are now focused on producing big blockbusters, action films, and animated films. They're looking for franchise-able

properties, so that their huge marketing investment can generate revenues on more than just one movie and can also expand into gaming, books, merchandise, licensing, and promotional revenues.

The number of films produced by the Hollywood studios has also decreased significantly over the last ten years from 179 in 2004 to 114 in 2013, a 36% decrease. Conversely, for the same period, independent films releases went from 310 to 545, an increase of 76%. (See table 5 below)

Table 5 Films Released 2004-2013
Source MPAA 2013

Films Released
Sources: Rentrak Corporation – Box Office Essentials (Total), MPAA (Subtotals)

	2004	2005	2006	2007	2008	2009	2010	2011	2012	2013	13 vs. 12	13 vs. 04
Films released[19]	489	507	594	611	638	557	563	609	677	659	-3%	35%
- 3D film releases[20]	2	6	8	6	8	20	26	45	40	45	13%	n/a
MPAA member total	179	194	204	189	168	158	141	141	128	114	-11%	-36%
- MPAA studios	100	113	124	107	108	111	104	104	94	84	-11%	-16%
- MPAA studio subsidiaries	79	81	80	82	60	47	37	37	34	30	-12%	-62%
Non-members	310	313	390	422	470	399	422	468	549	545	-1%	76%

[17] Note that films may be rated or re-rated months or even years after production. Includes non-theatrical films.
[18] Member studios include: Walt Disney Studios Motion Pictures, Paramount Pictures Corporation, Sony Pictures Entertainment, Inc. Twentieth Century Fox Film Corporation, Universal City Studios LLC, and Warner Bros. Entertainment Inc.
[19] Source: Rentrak Corporation – Box Office Essentials. Includes all titles that **opened** in 2013 that earned any domestic box office in the year. Historical data is regularly updated by Rentrak.
[20] 2012 3D film release figure was revised upward to include non-wide release films.

22

The reduction in the number of studio films over the last few years has created a void, a gap of sorts, for exhibitors and theatre chains. They cannot operate theatres just on studio films anymore; they need films to come out every week, and the studios are not filling the gap. This has enabled independent films with high commercial value to break through between big opening weekends for blockbusters.

The traditional studio model is gone
In the last couple of years, studios have gradually ceased their historical development deals with many producers. Many producers were on studio payrolls and benefitted from office space on the studio's back lot while

they were developing new film projects for that particular major. Very often, when the developed project would not interest that studio, it would end up in "turnaround" where it could potentially be picked up by another company for the equivalent of the development costs and some interests. That development model has become significantly less popular with studios.

The other characteristic of the six movie studios is their huge back lots filled with sound stages and exterior locations. The demand for those facilities are also decreasing in part because of the multiple government incentives in place in various US states and in many countries around the world, but also because special effects have become increasingly computerized. Over time, studios have sold part of their back lot real estate, but for most of them, they still face significant overheads, which are often passed on to film projects.

If you invest in a slate of films with a Hollywood studio, you may want to hire an expert to look into all the possible expenses that the studio may apply to your projects and ensure all these charges are justified, competitively priced and laid out contractually.

Studios need to reinvent their business model, improve their development efficiencies, reduce their overheads, mitigate their risks, and generate revenues from their soundstage and back lots through production services. By knowing this, you'll understand their objective to extract fees wherever they can to absorb all their overheads and you will have more insight to negotiate a deal that is fair and reasonable.

Stars are more grounded

Actor compensation has also changed. Gone are the days when most stars could ask for huge fees and be very selective. A handful of actors are still commanding premium salaries but their number has gradually diminished because of the decrease in big studio films and the proliferation of animated films. In recent years, big actors have increasingly worked for "scale" (i.e. the minimum Screen Actors Guild rate) on projects they really like, settling instead for profit participation. The first actor to do this was James Steward back in the 50s. Nowadays, this model is gaining traction, and that represents an opportunity for independent filmmakers to attract a recognizable and talented actor they otherwise would not be able to get, one whose clout and following will bolster the chances of succeeding.

Talent agencies are adapting to the new reality

Talent agencies are involved in film financing nowadays and must also adjust to the disruptive changes sweeping the industry. Each big agency has developed a branch that specializes in assembling financing for film projects in order for their talent pool (actors, writers and directors) to work and earn fees, for which they collect a 10% agent fee.

It's common knowledge now that a serious talent agency wouldn't be able to survive strictly on theatrical revenues. Over the last decade, television revenues have increased significantly and high quality drama series are now proliferating. TV executives have been successful in attracting great talent to the small screen and developed compelling, often edgy storytelling in particular on premium and cable networks. Therefore talent agencies eye revenue streams from television to make a sustainable profit. Cinema actors and television actors used to be working in silos. Expect the silos to break even more in the coming years. The same phenomenon is emerging with online video talent migrating to television and cinema.

Investors should use caution when they are represented by a talent agency simply to avoid a conflict (or appearance thereof) of interest if the agency is also representing directly or indirectly other interests such as talent or other financiers in the transaction. Keep in mind that the primary driver of the talent agency revenue model is to get their talent employed at the highest rate possible. If as a film financier, your strategy is to get talent at the most reasonable cost, and you're advised by a talent agency with its own talent involved in the transaction, you may be contending with a conflict of interest of sorts. You want to have someone who is independently advising you and who has your sole interests in mind. That being said, talent agents are often formidable partners for packaging film projects with writers, directors, actors and sometimes investors.

Crowd funding: the new trend for raising seed money and awareness

Another recent industry change is crowd funding or crowd sourcing. At this point, it hasn't significantly changed the way commercial films are financed, but I believe that it could be a way to trigger the first money in a project and to be able to secure talent contractually, so that a project can move to the next step of securing pre-sales out of international markets.

Although there is a place for crowd funding with donations, I have reservations about the equity crowd funding model and the producer's ability to interact with so many small investors in an effective way. In any situation I think a producer will always prefer to have some bigger, more seasoned, more experienced investors supporting his project and therefore reduce the number of interactions with investors in order to expedite the decision process. I also think that once crowd funding and crowd sourcing websites or platforms are allowed to give their contributors some profit participation, the management of all these agreements will become quite complex if not chaotic. It remains to be seen if such models will serve as a viable source of financing for bigger budget films.

A new wave of film entrepreneurs

Another change in the industry is the new wave of young, business-savvy film financiers and filmmakers. They understand that the business drivers of their project should not be overlooked. Megan Ellison, Shivani Rawat, Ken Kao, Nicolas Chartier, Michael Benaroya: these are some examples of people having entered the film industry being properly advised and understanding the magnitude of the risk that they are ready to take.

Exhibition windows are squeezed

One of the constant changes in the film industry is the pressure applied on what we call the windows of exhibition of a feature film (see table 6 below).

Table 6 Example of various orderly and sequential exhibition windows for feature films.

Release Date - Month 3	Month 3 - 6	Month 4+	Month 5+	Year 1	Year 3+
Theatrical Release	Airlines Hotels Video-On-Demand (VOD)	Home Media (DVD, Blu-ray and digital downloads)	Pay per view	Pay TV & Subscription Video on demand (SVOD) Netflix	Broadcast network and basic cable

The entertainment industry has experienced many disruptive technology changes during recent years such as Pay-per-View (PPV), Video on Demand (VOD), Subscription Video on Demand (SVOD) services like HBONow and HBOGo, Hulu, Netflix, etc., personal video recorders (PVRs) such as Tivo, as well as the proliferation of smart phones and tablets. Each technology creates some form of pressure on the existing orderly windows of exhibition. Each new player in the industry demands a quicker access to entertainment from the theatrical release. These windows and blackout periods are all part of lengthy, complex negotiations where rights holders try to avoid creating any dangerous precedent.

The theatrical window has seen its share of pressure, but exhibitors are still a powerful force capable of preventing high-profile films from being released "day and date" in

51

theaters and home media simultaneously. There have been a handful of films with a day and date release but they remain the exception. In any event, in the next five years, theaters will likely be forced to redefine their consumer experience to adjust to the new reality of entertainment, where large 3D flat screens are becoming more available and where younger generations consume and generate entertainment content seamlessly on multiple screens. In order for the theaters to remain competitive and attractive, exhibitors will explore new pricing and try to provide more a compelling offer (better seats, better food and beverages) to make the movie going experience unique and compelling.

Studios are experts at maximizing revenue in each window. Generally, we can expect the home media (DVD, VOD) window to offer films closer to the time of theatrical release because it will become more and more significant in terms of revenue for the studios. However, the theatrical release of a film is still today, and for the foreseeable future, the best way to raise awareness for a film, and to therefore trigger substantial revenues in each window thereafter.

It is improbable to successfully open a blockbuster only with social media and without television support. You still need significant efforts in P&A to get people to the theatre on Friday night to see your film and the risk is that, in the event the film is disappointing, the proliferation of social media tools such as Facebook and Twitter will allow the word to spread so fast that your film will die by the end of Friday night. Even if it's risky, a theatrical is still the best way to build awareness on your film that will increase the value of your film for the subsequent windows of exhibition.

Conclusion for chapter 3

- The filmed entertainment industry is not correlated to the bond and equity markets, making it an interesting alternative investment in a balanced portfolio.

- International markets are fueling most of the industry growth.
- The conversion of screens to digital is progressing rapidly.
- Studios produce less but bigger budget films while independent producers are increasing volume.
- Studios distribute independent films to generate incremental revenue, amortize operating costs and maintain a consistent output of products to exhibitors.
- Actors and talent agencies are adapting to new compensation models where they get a smaller upfront and a bigger piece of the backend.
- Crowd funding is emerging as a way to finance smaller films and raise development money.
- New, young and wealthy entrepreneurs are joining the industry often from real estate and technology.
- Traditional windows of exhibition of film are under pressure but so far, the bulk of films released still aim at a decent scale theatrical release to generate returns.
- Social media alone is still not sufficient to open a film on a large scale; TV ads are still essential.

"It takes as much energy to wish as it does to plan"

–Eleanor Roosevelt

Chapter 4
The Filmmaking Process from an Investor's Perspective: Follow the Money

As a film investor, you need to understand the fundamental steps of the filmmaking process. It will help you navigate through contracts, budgets, and financial structures, and it will allow you to fully appreciate the complexity and the many pieces that come together to make a film project successful.

There are four phases in the development and production of a film; development, preproduction, production (or principal photography), postproduction, and they always follow the same order. (See table 7 below).

Table 7. Timeline for typical development and production of a feature film (in months)

Development																	
Pre story acquisition						Acquisition			Script evolution, drafts rewrites and polishes								
1	2	3	4	5	6	7	8	9	10	11	12	13	14	15	16	17	18

Development					Principal			Postproduction									
Finance and sales plan				Preproduction	Photography												
19	20	21	22	23	24	25	26	27	28	29	30	31	32	33	34	35	36

Once the film is completed, the next step is distribution, and we will devote a whole chapter to it. But for now, let's take a closer look at each phase, but from an investor's perspective.

Development: The first obstacles

The development part is the phase of honing a screenplay from an original idea, a book, a true story, to arrive at what we call a "packaged script". This is where the idea will be developed, the underlying property acquired. The writing process includes various outlines, treatments, and screenplays in different drafts, rewrites and polishes. During development, a chain of title will be documented to support the ownership of the intellectual property (IP).

In parallel, physical production prep will start and budgeting will be undertaken. The budget has two distinct sections: above the line (ATL) and below the line (BTL). ATL costs are related to the screenplay, the key talent. They are separated from the rest as they are linked to distinctive creative forces of the film that often command variable fees depending who is "attached" to the project. BTL expenses comprise all other costs such as technical crews, equipment, post-production, general administration, etc.

Once a budget is determined, the producer will look at all the financial resources at his disposal to meet that budget. They include: government incentives for shooting the film in specific states or countries (often called soft money because it does not have to be repaid); deferments[7] from talent and vendors (fees that will only become payable once a certain breakeven is reached); pre-licensing contracts that can be financed at a discount rate by a senior lender, unsold

---

7 A deferment is a sum that is payable to a writer or performer, director producer, or someone else connected to the film, out of the revenues derived from the exploitation of the film, typically after the deduction of some distribution fees and expenses. It is usually after the financiers and the bond company have recovered the full sum they advanced for the cost of production and delivery of the film.

international territories that can be can leveraged by a mezzanine/subordinated debt lender, called gap financing and equity money, which is often required in the first place to persuade the key actors and director to commit to the project.

Once the financing has been structured and the capital sources confirmed, a due diligence phase will be necessary before all parties can proceed with closing the financing and green lighting the production. The closing takes generally more time than anticipated, as issues rose by stakeholders often need to be addressed by one or more parties.

As you can see from the table, development is a tedious phase and it generally takes 2 years in the process. Some very successful films have been in development for 7 to 10 years. It is a long road to secure all the elements necessary to close the financing of a film.

Preproduction: Measure twice. Cut once.

The second phase is pre-production. This is a critical phase where all of the proper planning for the very costly principal photography phase should take place. The planning phase is integral to achieving the plan.

As I often like to say, "Remember the 9 Ps":
Proper
Planned
Pre-
Production
Prevents
Poor
Performance in
Principal
Photography.

If your producer botches the pre-production, I can guarantee that the costs will rise during production and efficiency will suffer. Usually, pre-production will last 6-12 weeks, during which a professional producer will break down the script into scenes and identify locations, props, cast members, costumes, special effects and visual effects. He will create a detailed schedule to coordinate the availability of all necessary elements for each day of shooting. He will organize reading sessions with talent, key crew and department heads. He will supervise the construction of sets, hire crews and make sure that the financiers agree to a cash flow draw down schedule for the next phases based on a predetermined start date for principal photography.

Principal Photography: the crucial and costly phase

Of course, production, which typically lasts 6-12 weeks, is the phase of physical film production that involves the actual filming of the story, whether it's on location and/or in various sound stages. Each day is scheduled tightly around scenes, factoring in the involvement of actors, extras and making smart use of different locations and crews. Most of the costs will be incurred during principal photography and the draw down schedule of the financial package should reflect that. The cash available for the film is usually disbursed by the completion guarantor to the producer based on that draw down schedule to ensure proper controls and uses of funds. As you can imagine, many risks are involved during principal photography, namely the availability of the film's essential elements (actors, director), the weather, and labor disputes to name a few. Every risk should be identified in advance and mitigation measures should be put in place to avoid delays or shutdowns. The Chapter 12 of this book will give you specific examples of risks related to independent films.

One of Hollywood's most cited directing styles belongs to Clint Eastwood, who has directed more than 30 movies. In his early years as an actor, Eastwood was apparently frustrated when scenes were being re-shot multiple times. As a director, he became famous for his ability to efficiently reduce the amount of takes needed and to keep budgets under control. He usually completes most scenes on the first take.

Post-production: towards the finishing line

The fourth phase is postproduction, where the raw material (dailies) shot during principal photography is edited into a complete feature film. That includes picture editing, sound editing, composing and recording the score, music editing, adding visual special effects, adding audio sound effects such as Automated Dialogue Replacement (ADR), Foley (post-synchronized sound effects), sound design, sound mixing, color correction, titles design, and negative cutting. With the plethora of technology available today, post-production can help reduce costs of producing a film. Conversely, post-production costs are sometimes overlooked or underestimated by the producer. Again tracking costs before and during post-production can make a big difference for an investor.

Film production compared to commercial real estate

Many high net worth individuals and hedge funds are familiar with the different phases of real estate development, which bear some similarities to film production. (See table 8 below)

As in a large real estate transaction, the investor and his representative should make sure every measure is taken to protect his capital and maximize his return in each of these phases.

Table 8: Film Production vs. Real Estate, R. Kiratsoulis, 2011.

FILM PRODUCTION	REAL ESTATE
DEVELOPMENT	DEVELOPMENT
1. Generally, this phase occurs when the producer selects a film project (i.e., original screenplay, adaptation based on a novel, inspired by an idea, short story, comic character, etc.) 2. Typically, the producer negotiates with the rights holder a purchase option for an	1. Generally, this phase occurs when the developer selects a property site for a proposed commercial building project. 2. Typically the developer negotiates with the owner of the property a purchase option for an agreed upon purchase price and specified period of time during which the

FILM PRODUCTION	REAL ESTATE
agreed upon purchase price and specified period of time for the original screenplay and underlying rights, if applicable, to be exercised. 3. Generally, the producer and director (if attached) collaborate with the screenwriter to the extent necessary (i.e., rewrites or dialogue polishes), and finalize the screenplay in a form ready to submit to an independent production company or studio for the next step in the "value chain".	option must be exercised.
PRE-PRODUCTION 1. Generally, this phase entails the producer hiring a casting director and attaching the principal creative elements to the project by making "pay or play" offers to the director and principal and supporting cast (above the line costs); and attaching key crew elements (i.e., below the line costs: Line Producer, Director of Photography, Production Manager, Art Director, Production Designer, Editor, Music Composer, Production Accountant, etc.) 2. Typically, the producer will have a preliminary production shooting schedule, budget, and cash flow drawdown prepared; secure bids and quotations from outside vendors for the physical production costs (i.e., below the line: camera, transportation, grip, lighting & electric, catering, insurance, film laboratory, etc.), and select locations and/or sound stages for the film to be shot. 3. Obtaining Letters of Intent from financing institutions & completion guarantor, entering into pre-sale distribution agreements, negative pick-up agreements , and production service arrangements to be utilized as collateral in finalizing the production.	**PLANNING** 1. Generally, this phase entails the developer proceeding to file for local zoning, entitlements, and other governmental permits; and selecting an architect, for the various design and construction specifications of the proposed commercial building. 2. Typically, the developer hires a construction supervisor to work in conjunction with the architect in securing construction bids and quotations from general contractors and sub-contractors for the construction schedule, preparation of the construction budget, and cash flow drawdown schedule; and negotiates with a financial institution and completion guarantor for the interim construction financing for the proposed building project. 3. Typically, during this phase, the developer will hire a leasing agent to commence pre-leasing of rental space to proposed tenants.
PRINCIPAL PHOTOGRAPHY 1. Generally, this phase entails the actual physical filming of the screenplay on location and on sound stages, if necessary. 2. During this phase cost reports are prepared weekly by the Production Accountant with full explanations for any significant cost variances and/or overruns	**CONSTRUCTION** 1. Generally, this phase is marked by awarding the contract to a general building contractor and commencing with preparation of site excavation and the physical construction of the basic building structure. 2. During this phase of construction, cost

FILM PRODUCTION	REAL ESTATE
which are primarily monitored by the producer and completion guarantor.	reports are prepared weekly by the Construction Accountant with full explanations provided for any significant cost variances and/ or overruns which are primarily monitored by the developer and completion guarantor.
POST-PRODUCTION 1. Generally, this phase entails the late stages of film production after principal photography, including editing, dubbing, adding music, special effects, digital intermediate, and main and end titles. 2. Typically, this period is marked by completion of the film and the preparation by the film laboratory of all mandatory delivery items (i.e., answer print, interpositive, internegative, video master, optical and M&E tracks, key art and trailer) which are necessary to complete delivery and commercially distribute the feature film worldwide.	**IMPROVEMENTS & BETTERMENTS** 1. Generally, this phase entails the late stages of finishing the interior non-structural construction of the commercial building and includes the various interior embellishments to the building primarily involving tenant improvements and betterments (e.g., dry wall, lighting, carpentry, wall covering, carpeting, etc.), which are necessary to physically complete the leased premises prior to tenant occupancy.
DISTRIBUTION 1. Generally, during this final phase the feature film is delivered to domestic and foreign distributors, and thereafter revenues commence to be received from the commercial exploitation of the film. 2. Typically all revenues received by the collection agent during this phase are repaid to financiers (i.e., P&A and Production) as agreed upon in priority order of recoupment as contractually provided under an interparty or intercreditor agreement; and any and all amounts received in excess thereof are paid to the guilds, gross participants, deferees, producers, and financiers of the film.	**LEASING & MORTGAGE FINANCING** 1. Generally, this final phase is marked by the completion of the commercial building including all related tenant improvements, and leasing the vacant tenant space not previously preleased during the planning and construction phases. 2. Typically, during this phase the developer negotiates for a "takedown" permanent mortgage to repay the interim construction debt incurred during the Planning stage.

Front loaded investment

The cost of producing the film is incurred during the first four phases: development, preproduction, production, and postproduction. However, the revenue generation will only happen in the distribution phase. The filmmaking process would be completely pointless if there was no distribution: the domestic and international exploitation of the film. Without it, there is no audience, no revenue, no profit, no impact.

We talked about windows before, but let's summarize the timeline of a typical film for its exploitation or exhibition. (See table 9 below)

Table 9 Typical schedule of film revenues and expenses with recoupment horizon per type of financing.

Typical schedule of feature film revenues and expenses with recoupment horizon per type of financing																							
Year 1				Year 2				Year 3				Year 4				Year 5				Year 6			
Q1	Q2	Q3	Q4	Q1	Q2	Q3	Q4	Q1	Q2	Q3	Q4	Q1	Q2	Q3	Q4	Q1	Q2	Q3	Q4	Q1	Q2	Q3	Q4

Expenses — Revenues

Development — Preproduction, Production & Postproduction — Theatrical Release — Airlines, Hotels & VOD — Home Media (DVD, Bluray and digital downloads) — Pay per View — Pay TV (including Netflix) — Broadcast network & basic cable

Bridge — Senior lender — P&A — Subordinated Debt (Mezz) — Equity investor

So your recoupment timeline will be shorter or longer depending on when and how you invest in the film project, whether at the beginning of the process as an equity partner or later on as a bridge lender, senior lender, subordinated lender or P&A lender.

As you know, time is money, so if your capital is at work for a longer period of time, your return should be adjusted accordingly.

A film is a collaborative effort

A typical film production requires cooperation from many people. The various stakeholders come from different areas: bankers, producers, lenders, bond companies, talent, talent agencies, sales agents and collection agencies, entertainment lawyers, film financing advisors, distributors, theatres, marketers, merchandisers, licensees, branded entertainment experts, financiers, government personnel, vendors, etc.

For a film to succeed, all of these stakeholders need to work hand in hand, understand each other's interests and move in the same direction led by a solid producer. The producer is the person who holds it all together. He is responsible for execution from script to screen.

Now that we have clarified the four phases of the film production process, let's focus a little more on the financing activities that are specific to the independent film production process.

Ways to help financing an independent film

In order to raise the money to finance a film, a producer has many options and tools.

Deferments

The first tool is a deferment[8]. A deferment may come in very handy while setting up the financing of a film - as it allows for a portion of the sum due to a stakeholder to only be paid once a certain negotiated threshold is met. The postponed "back-end" payment inherent in a deferral is an excellent tool that takes risk into account and allows the budget and the film itself to make more financial and commercial sense.

---

[8] The threshold for the payment of the deferment varies greatly. It sometimes coincides with the breakeven point or after the point where equity investors have recouped their capital and/or premium.

Bank financing
Collateralized bank financing is also available, which requires you have qualifying tax credits from a solid institution, as well as pre-licensing agreements with a reputable sales agent in foreign territories. These elements can be financed with a certain discount by a bank at a reasonable rate.

Gap (mezzanine/subordinated debt) loans
There's also gap and super gap financing. Gap is also called subordinated debt financing or mezzanine financing, and is usually capped at 20% of the whole budget. This type of loan is based essentially on the value of the unsold international territories, which makes it a riskier loan and therefore entails a higher yield that the senior debt.

Super gap loans
Super gap loans are those which comprise 20-40% of the budget. Super gap is even more risky because it bets on completing a higher degree of future sales and, as you can easily imagine, commands higher interest charges and fees than gap.

Soft money
Soft monies are sources of funds that producers don't need to repay, such as grants, government subsidies, rebates, tax credits, or co production benefits. Tax incentives are applicable to preproduction, production or postproduction phases. Keep in mind that some refundable tax credits are preferable to transferrable tax credits because the latter will usually require a broker to sell the tax credit a discount to a third party who has capital gains in the same territorial jurisdiction where the credit is granted.

Equity
Then you have "hard monies": capital in the form of equity investments from the proceeds of the film. Equity investors risk not getting their money back for lack of

performance and, as such, deserve a pre-negotiated return that is adjusted to their risk. Generally, an equity investor fronting the capital all by himself will obtain a 20% premium on his capital, an executive producer fee at closing of the financing and 50% of the net profits of the film for its entire life.

Branded entertainment

Finally, another source of financing is branded entertainment, commonly known as product integration and product placement, whereby a producer will either integrate a brand in the storyline of a film for a fee (product integration) or use the brand on the screen and will get the product for free for use during principal photography (product placement).

Product integration revenue is more difficult to obtain beforehand because the brand manager will often require a signed domestic distribution contract up front with at least 2,000 print or screens commitment and around $20 million of commitment for P&A budget. The brand manager wants to know that the movie will be distributed so that potential customers will likely see their brand.

The importance of an inter-party agreement

During the financing phase, many contracts will be drafted and negotiated between the producer and various stakeholders. They often impact each other by affecting the recoupment schedule. An inter-party agreement will be negotiated to regulate the relationship between various financing parties to a film. It is an important document that any financier in a film project should review thoroughly.

Collection Account Management (CAM)

Typically, a collection agency is appointed to collect the proceeds from the exploitation of the film and distribute them to the financiers, the producer and other beneficiaries, such as deferees and profit participants, in accordance with directions set out in the Collection Management agreement. That agency should be independent and the distribution of the collected proceeds should be straightforward based on the CAM agreement, which instructs the sales agent to have all revenues paid in the collection account, and instructs the agency, which acts as a trusted third party, on the allocation and disbursement of those revenues. A collection account (bank account) is opened, into which the worldwide revenues of the film must be paid.

The complexity of financial reporting for an independent film

The definition of net profit is never standard and is always determined contractually. Since various participants in the same project can utilize different definitions of net profit, the producer will have to create a series of financial reports for the payment of these participants based on each agreement. Producers have their own set of accounting books based on agreed accounting principles, and one for their partners. Finally, the producer will also produce reports for tax purposes. That's one of the reasons why we often hear people say that producers, distributors and studios have many books. (In chapter 9, we will cover the distribution issues more in depth.)

Conclusion Chapter 4

- There are four phases in the production of a film; development, pre-production, production (i.e. principal photography) and post-production.
- Pre-production is a crucial phase to save time and money during principal photography.
- Post-production is often under estimated as a cost center in the budget.
- There are various ways to help finance a film: deferments, bank loans on presales and tax incentives, brand integration, gap financing and equity.

- The flow of monies in a film project will follow a certain process going out and coming in similar to a commercial real estate project.

- Revenue will only materialize at the distribution phase once the film is completed. Without distribution, no revenue.

- As an investor, you should always have a clear understanding of the cash flows before committing your capital. The Collection Account Management agreement and the inter-party agreement dictate how money flows between the various stakeholders in the film finance structure.

- Once your capital is deployed, it is also important to track production costs and distribution revenue to increase your chances of recouping and making a profit.

"Innovation distinguishes between a leader and a follower."

–Steve Jobs

Chapter 5
Most Profitable Selective Film investment Types
A Closer Look

The financing needs of a film producer will vary greatly depending on the process phase he is in and its cash flow requirements.

In the previous chapters, we have seen that there are various types of capital used in the financing of a film.

Senior Debt
The first is the senior debt, which is typically provided by a bank or a financial institution. Basically, the bank will cash flow from 50% to 80% of the presales contracts receivables and tax incentives from the government. The senior lender is always looking for receivables: contracts from bankable sources. These contracts will generally be reassigned to the bank until the bank is fully refunded. The bank will of course require a repayment of its principal and a reasonable interest charge. No profit or rights will divert to the bank as senior lenders.

Mezzanine Debt
The second category is mezzanine lender or subordinate lender[9]; sometimes people call them "gap

---

[9] In a nutshell, subordinate debt financing or mezzanine financing is an intermediate terminal, typically 12-24 months, which is advanced to a production borrower which is generally collateralized by a second priority security interest in the mortgage of copyright and also by an assignment of proceeds from the film. So generally the financier agrees to subordinate its collateral security interest in the film to a senior lender, usually a bank, whereby upon the payment of the senior loan, the financier sublets or substitutes into the contractual rights

financiers" because they finance the missing gap in the financial structure. The word "mezzanine" refers to the fact that this loan is situated below the senior debt but higher in priority than equity. This is a much riskier loan but it also carries a higher yield than that of senior debt as well a small portion of the back-end profits. Basically the mezzanine lender is advancing funds towards international sales estimates or "unsold territories". If the senior lender has also financed 80-90 percent of the tax credits, the subordinated lender often counts the remaining 10-20 percent of those unfinanced tax credits as an additional sum of collateral.

Because of its inherent risk in financing unsold territories, a subordinated debt transaction requires a thorough assessment of the project's creative merits and a conservative valuation of each unsold territory.

The additional risk is that if the completed film doesn't sell as well as anticipated and if certain presales were difficult to collect by the bank who provided the senior debt, that bank may sell other unsold territories for less in order to get its money back, leaving with you with less revenue for your own recoupment.

Equity financing
The third category of financing is equity financing, where the investor in equity will provide cash for a portion of profits and possible rights and ownership. Typically the producer will negotiate a premium, or a return to the investor of 20%, and will be ready to give 50% of net profits to that equity investor if he funded 100% of the film production

---

previously rendered to the senior lender, and in consideration for providing the subordinate debt financing, the investor will have a one-time financing fee, an estimated interest reserve for the first 12-18 months of the loan, an executive producer fee, and also a legal allowance along with a meaningful profit participation in the film in certain instances. This type of film financing is consequently advanced to the production borrower only upon completion of the final production financing, and it requires also the issuance of a completion bond designating the subordinate debt holder as a loss paid beneficiary in the event that the film is not completed by the bonded delivery date.

budget, while the other 50% remain with the producer. In most instances, if a producer gives some net points to talent or other stakeholders, these points will come from his own share of 50%. Again, everything is possible provided it is stipulated clearly in the agreement. Remember: there are no standard, one-size-fits-all definitions in film financing agreements.

Generally the bank acts as a senior lender and the subordinate debt lender will be looking at international sales revenues to refund its loan. The bank is advancing funds based on receivables that will be re-assigned to the bank. If you expect to be refunded from domestic, it entails an even greater risk because you have no control over the release date and schedule, the weather, the number of theaters and screens that will show your film, and the P&A budget necessary to market the film, which is never included in the production budget of the film.

P&A Financing
Some people will be willing to lend money - at a premium - to either the distributor or the producer to finance the P&A budget necessary to release the film. P&A includes prints and digital copies of the film and the all-important advertising campaigns to reach the audience and entice them to go to the movies on a Friday night. This P&A loan will be refunded in priority from domestic receipts, once the distributor takes his average 25 to 30 percent distribution fee from the gross rentals received from theatres.

Bridge Financing
Bridge financing is a short time loan that is not protected by a completion bond, and therefore is riskier. Bridge financing may be necessary when some costs need to be fronted before the financing of a film "closes." Often this happens when a "pay or play[10]" contract obligation with an

---

[10] A pay or play contract is a commitment to pay a director or performer made before production commences, and sometimes before all the finance has become

actor or a director forces the producer to start shooting scenes. The loan is repaid with a premium when the financing of the film closes.

As you can see in Table 10 below, each type of investment carries a risk-adjusted return. These returns are just for example purposes as each rate and each fee is subject to negotiations.

Table 10. Example of returns and recoupment horizon per type of film investment

Type	Risk	Approximate Return[11]		Recoupment Horizon
Bridge Loan	Very High	Highest	25% Interest & fees	1-6 months
Bank Loan	Lowest	Lowest	5-7% interest & fees	12-18 months
Tax Incentives	Low	Medium	15-20% interest	6-15 months
Subordinated/ Gap /Mezz	Medium-High	Medium -High	20-25% Interest & fees +Backend	18-24 months
P&A Loan	Medium-High	Medium -High	20-25% Interest & fees	6-12 months
Equity	Highest	High	20% premium +50% of backend	3-5 yrs

Territorial Acquisition Financing

Occasionally, selective territorial acquisition (or carve out) can be used to finance a film early in the process. A producer may carve out and sell a specific territory to an investor before the film is offered to a foreign sales agent. That investor may exploit those rights through its other

---

unconditional, regardless of whether his or her services are used.

[11] Most rates are based on LIBOR London Interbank offered rate.

businesses or simply expects to resell them at a premium once the film is completed.

The International "Waterfall" Recoupment

To really understand what a "waterfall" means, one has to look at the international sales recoupment schedule for a waterfall.

- The collection account management fees and expenses are usually first out.

- Then, the sales agency will take its sales fee, which can vary from 7.5% to 11.5% for films with a budget under $10,000,000 and can go to 3.5-5% for films over $20,000,000 budget. Depending on negotiations with the senior financier, some or all of the fee may be deferred until the debt has been recouped.

- Then come the sales expenses, whereby a sales agent will deduct any fees to attend sales market. There are four sales markets that sales agency utilize to present films to foreign buyers: the European Film Market in Berlin in February, the Cannes Film Market in May, the Toronto Film Festival in September, and the American Film Market of Santa Monica in early November. As an investor, check the dates of the film market. If your sales agent is only going to attend Toronto and Santa Monica to sell the film, the marketing costs should be significantly lower compared to attending Berlin or Cannes. Investors try to cap the sales expenses since they're generally non-refundable.

- The third person to be repaid is the senior lender, or the bank loan.

- Once the bank loan is refunded, the next person in line to recoup is usually the subordinate lender, or the mezzanine lender.

- Fifth are typically residuals, in the United States, from the DGA (Directors Guild of America), the WGA (Writers Guild of America), or IATSE (International Alliance of Theatrical Stage Employees). The position on residuals will depend on the deal. While the senior lender - if an established bank, but not if a private fund - will generally go ahead of the guilds, the guilds will recoup ahead of everyone else unless a residuals reserve has been created as part of the financing requirements. Many producers need to follow negotiated custodial agreements to pay residuals on selective markets and windows. Often, the sales agent collects the residuals and remits them to the guilds.

- Then the completion guarantor will be refunded if he incurred unbudgeted costs; otherwise the guarantor will not be entitled to recoup money, as its fee has been paid for in the budget.

- In seventh position, there may be other recoupment, e.g., shortfalls related to the tax credits or deferments of producers and other key personnel.

- Finally, the producer and the equity investors will be refunded.

The Domestic "Waterfall" Recoupment

The domestic box office number often reported in trade magazines and newspapers represents the total dollar amount generated by the film; however, people forget that nearly 50% of that amount will remain with the theatre chains.

- So the first 50% of box office stays with exhibitors

- They will remit the other 50%, called the theatrical rentals, to a distributor that has the rights on the film in North America.

- From that 50% the distributor will keep its own distribution fee that averages 25%.

- Distributors will then use the available proceeds to repay the P&A budget for the film
- Only then will the distributor start to pay back the production cost by sending the remaining money to the producer and the equity investor to recoup the production budget or what is called the "negative cost[12]".

However, most films don't fully recoup their cost just from the theatrical window unless they are high revenue and low cost, such as the "Paranormal Activity" franchise[13].

The longer the recoupment... the higher the fees.
Other windows of exhibition will be necessary for the film budget (negative cost) to be totally recouped. Keep in mind, though, that in each window the distribution company will take various types of fees and deduct direct expenses and a portion of their overhead. Experienced financiers always look for these hidden costs and fees to make sure they are reasonable and customary. To that end, a financial advisor can sometimes help you generate savings at the negotiation stage by eliminating some of these fees or reducing their impact.

Conclusion Chapter 5
- Each type of investments carries different risk profiles and yields.
- Depending on the investor's comfort level of risk and the project's specific qualities, a thorough assessment can be made by an experienced independent advisor to help the investor protect his capital and improve his chances of getting a favorable ROI.

---

[12] The negative cost term refers to the film negative which becomes the final tangible asset after the film is produced.
[13] Paranormal Activity's first four films' average budget was $2,241,667 and generated an average domestic box office of $58,433,477, per the-numbers.com.

- Often mezzanine loans and P&A loans are interesting investment vehicles provided that the projects are carefully handpicked and manages by reputable producers and sales agents.

"The four most expensive words in the English language are, 'This time it's different.' "

–Sir John Templeton

Chapter 6
The Systematic Approach of Successful Investors:
Don't Fall In Love!

It may be useful for readers to look at how successful investors generally approach a film financing opportunity. Investors that have an appetite for the industry will conduct a search of projects, based on specific criteria. The successful investors always stick to those criteria in each project assessment. They may be flexible but before they decide to break one of their "rules" they want to know why they should do so and what is the upside.

A great story well told

They look for a great story well told – a screenplay that is very compelling in a given genre. We will cover that very concept in the next chapter.

They know what sells

Film investors will usually look at a specific genre or a couple of genres of films based on their appeal and their historical track record. The film genres are as follows: adventure, action, drama, comedy, thriller/suspense, horror, romantic comedy (rom-com), musical, documentary, and black comedy. Successful investors need to have their antennae out there and make sure that the good projects will come to them. They often retain the services of independent advisors to be able to attract and sift through projects and come up with the best.

Most investors don't want to select projects that have been passed on by too many people, which in this industry can "burn" it, and you may end up not able to sell the project because it's already been presented in a previous version in a less appealing way. On the other hand, many popular films were initially declined, to the later embarrassment of the executive who opted not to pursue it, so judge carefully. In recent times, many film projects in the budget bracket between 20 Million and 65 Million dollars initially developed and ultimately overlooked by the studios are now being considered by a limited group of independent producers because of their commercial appeal in local and foreign markets.

The most popular genres are adventure, action, and drama, but for a given project, you have to look at the specific audience. Although there are more dramas made each year, they generate fewer revenues on average than adventure films.

A realistic budget
What is the budget for the film and how realistic and reasonable is it in relation to the genre? The most popular genres are often dictated by their international appeal, as producers tend to finance their film with international presales. Many film investors prefer the thriller/suspense/action/adventure genres because they can attract more significant presales from international markets.

A proven audience
What is the audience for such a film? What specific demographic segment will be attracted by this story and where is it located? Are these people easily drawn to theaters? What are the recent comparable films in that genre and their budget scope, and how did they perform at the box office?

A determined appetite for investment
One of the main criteria that an investor will have is an overall appetite for the amount of capital that he wants to spend, and the targeted risk-adjusted return on investment that he needs before he green lights an investment.

Investors need to determine if they want to place capital through equity or debt. This is one of the most strategic questions in this industry and, frankly, one that too many producers and financiers still overlook.

On one hand, as an equity investor, you have no predetermined amount that is owed to you in case of a revenue shortfall. You commit to invest at the early stage of the film development process, and your upside is a defined premium on your investment from the proceeds of the film once it reaches breakeven. Now given Secret Number One – that only a very small percentage of films released make a net profit – you are basically gambling on the domestic performance of the film, provided that the film is even good enough to get distributed domestically.

On the other hand, as a lender, you are entitled to a promissory note, a given interest charge, plus some fees and legal expenses allowance depending of the risk position and the quality of the collateral available against your loan for the production. But then again, if there are no revenues, there are no loan repayments and often no tangible assets to seize other than a film negative, and if you have a promissory note, you can eventually foreclose the film and own it until your debt is repaid.

What is the success rate of a senior lender in films? Probably around 90%, though keep in mind that their return is smaller because their risk is also smaller. As most senior lenders in film are a handful of banks, they have huge leverage to get repaid. A producer or a distributor in default of a payment to a bank would have a hard time getting any financing going forward.

Find the sweet spot
Between the senior lender at a relatively low return/low risk and the equity partner at a theoretically high return/high risk, there are often opportunities that some

investors have identified as the sweet spot. I'm talking about subordinate debt or mezzanine financing, prints and advertising financing, and bridge financing. There's also tax credit financing that can yield an interesting return with a moderate risk.

Assess the sales

Successful film investors also systematically assess the domestic sales potential, though this is one of the most difficult estimates. You have to base your assessment on comparables from the last five years: comparables in terms of budget, release, amplitude, the number of screens the film was released on, the season, the P&A budget, genre, and cast. You also need to have an appreciation of the ancillary revenues from each of these comparable films; it is not always easy to obtain, but it is possible.

Successful investors don't get fooled by vague comparables. Rather, they operate under a pessimistic scenario: they assess the story elements, audience, and profitability to see if this film can realistically secure domestic distribution when completed.

Independent advisory for a better alignment of interests

Smart financiers often require independent advice. We all know that the producer's job is to be the cheerleader for the project and be enthusiastic, so the investor should always retain independent advice because his capital is at risk and he needs to make his decision based on his own interest.

In my humble opinion, the advisor should be independent and should not be compensated solely if a transaction goes forward. The reason for this is quite simple; sometimes the advisor's work can be very significant in the decision to not go forward with a given investment, and he should be paid for his time and his work, even when he recommends that his client should keep his money for another opportunity. Some investors may be tempted to hire consultants or "finders" on a contingent compensation only, i.e., paid only on the commission of a transaction, but I suggest this is a risky short-term view on a very important capital investment decision. If the investor is serious about investing many millions of dollars in a film project, he should retain (for a relatively modest fee compared to the investment at stake) the service of an advisor that will be comfortable in advising him independently in the transaction beforehand. I know this sounds self-serving because I myself act as independent advisor. But you don't need to retain my services. Just use common business sense and get the independent advise you need if you are serious about investing for a decent ROI in this industry and feel that all measures possible have been taken to help preserve capital.

Diversify and be selective

Smart investors also spread their capital investment across more than one project. The proverb "never put all of your eggs in one basket" holds true for film investment. Although by allocating or diversifying your investment in more than one project helps spread and mitigate the risk, there is also a risk in being spread too thin and losing focus or "granularity" in each of the project-specific factors of success. A smart way to diversify is to select 3-5 projects that may or may not be related so that you multiply your chances of hitting a homerun if one of those films becomes a huge success.

Again I would suggest caution if investing in blind slates of films, where you let somebody else not perfectly aligned with your interests (i.e. a studio, a producer, a talent agency, etc.) decide which films will be financed, because you want to know the merit of each project on which you are risking capital. What guarantee would you have that you won't end up financing the riskier projects while the producer or agency keeps the most promising projects for themselves? You also should take a serious look at the potential consequences of cross collateralization of revenues when there is more than one film and how that plays out for you in terms of recoupment of your investment.

Size matters

Successful investors also know that certain types of investments require a minimum amount of capital. For instance, subordinated debt-financing transactions usually require $3-3.5 million because of the due diligence and the legal fees associated with the transaction; it is often not worth considering for a smaller amount. Conversely, sometimes it's worth considering co-investing with other financiers. That's definitely an option to access bigger projects, but the decision-making process has to be nimble and co-financiers need to have clear agreements on how they will recoup their money. Usually it will be *pari passu*, which means they will have equal importance in the recoupment.

Savvy investors don't "fall in love" with a project because they want to prevent their financial judgment from being influenced by emotion. That's why some investors prefer to have an advisor who will do the heavy lifting and allow for an "arm's length" interaction with the production company and director. One more reason to stick to a due diligence process, a topic we will cover in detail in Chapter 11.

Know your business partners

Understand who the key players are: the producer, the talent, the director and the senior lender. Find out what bank is being retained, what are the government incentives and whether they include refundable or transferable tax credits. Ask how the completion bond has been negotiated, and how the collection management agreement and the interparty agreement are structured. Understand the distribution situation (both domestically and internationally).

It is a fact that the producer's style of leadership and personality will affect everybody involved. This speaks volume to one of the most critical risks to assess: the execution risk. Investors have to make their own judgment of the team assembled before them and their ability to deliver the film effectively through a collaborative process.

Who's for real?

Unfortunately, there are many people in this industry pretending to have capital who, when the time comes to put the money forward, often lack the funds. One of the most famous scenes from the film "Jerry Maguire" starring Tom Cruise is when Cuba Gooding Jr. repeatedly exclaims "Show me the money, show me the money!" Vetting investors remains one of the biggest challenges for producers. Knowing for certain that the investor is serious and has the funds available is not always an easy task.

A financier's advantage: quick access to funds if necessary

The most successful financiers are able to show proof of funds quickly and, most importantly, to transfer the required funds into an escrow account expediently. From that moment on, provided that they have negotiated a proper escrow agreement, they operate from strength and are able to negotiate the best risk-adjusted returns because they come off as serious investors. To that effect, some financing companies charge a significant premium simply because they are able to close a transaction much faster than larger financial institutions.

No blank checks

Smart investors always act with proper caution, which means that they usually negotiate an escrow agreement before the money is put into escrow with the bond company. They have an independent team actively involved in a due diligence process on their behalf to ensure that all representations and obligations are verified, and that the preceding conditions are met.

They also know that the real work begins once the financing closes and their investment is disbursed. They know that they need to track costs to make sure that every dollar is spent wisely, properly, and that there is a concerted effort to do things in a cost-conscious, economical way, which we'll discuss in Chapter 12 and 12.5.

Able to say no

Successful film investors often love movies and are passionate about this industry. The best of them are generally not too vulnerable to the glitz or allure of stardom; they don't base their investment decisions on rubbing shoulders with stars, or being invited on set or to the film premiere. They know that every investor, good or bad, will be entitled to such perks if they invest in a film. That's the easy part. It's easy to say yes to that. The difficult part is to say "no" to people you appreciate about a project that is not as sound as it is presented or simply does not meet your investment criteria.

One of the things a smart investor will ask of a producer is a complete analysis, which includes the script breakdown, production boards, schedules, budgets, financial projections, global rights sales analysis, distribution windows, ancillary products, and license schedules, promotional tie-in lists, and marketing recommendations for or from a sales agent for distribution of foreign territories.

Conclusion Chapter 6

- Even if most good films involve the hero falling in love, investors know that falling in love with a film project can be hazardous.
- They have to base their investing decision on a fair and thorough assessment of the various risks before selecting the proper form of investments and negotiating the most favorable terms to mitigate the risk that they take.
- They understand what is selling in current markets.

- They determine if the budget is realistic and reasonable.
- They measure the audience potential of the film.
- They have a set of criteria for investing.
- They take a serious look at sales estimates and sales agents reports.
- They often retain independent advisors for larger transactions.
- They are very selective.
- They diversify into more than one project.
- They can afford to lose their investment but are very focused on capital preservation.
- They know and trust the producer.
- They show availabilities of funds quickly and disburse cautiously. No blank checks.
- They can say no. Passing on a project is OK.

"If you want to keep total creative control on your story in Hollywood, write a poem."

-

Unknown

Chapter 7
Start with a Great Story, Well Told

There are thousands and thousands of film projects out there that have limited commercial appeal. The subject of this book is film financing for highly commercial independent films. The first criterion for that commercial appeal – and, therefore, revenue potential - is spelled S-T-O-R-Y. This warrants a chapter unto itself.

Simply put, the story needs to be great. It should transport and entertain audiences in a new manner and leave a strong favorable impression on them. Ideally, it will follow a proven method of story telling.

The Hero's Journey: A timeless approach to storytelling
Since the dawn of humanity, storytelling has adapted an archetype called "The Hero's Journey". See Figure 1 below.

Figure 1 The Hero's Journey, according to Joseph Campbell

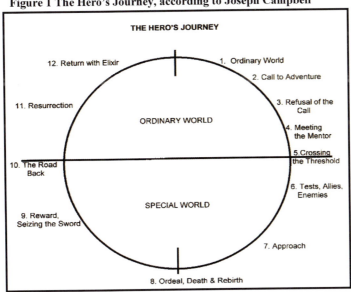

The hero's journey is what we call a "pattern of narrative" first described by Joseph Campbell, an American scholar that has appeared time and again in drama, oral storytelling, myth and all sorts of narrative forms. It describes the adventures of the protagonist (or the hero) who goes out and achieves something of great value for himself and/or a group of people that the audience cares about.

The story hero is introduced in his ORDINARY WORLD where he receives the CALL TO ADVENTURE. He's RELUCTANT at first to CROSS THE FIRST THRESHOLD where he eventually encounters TESTS, ALLIES and ENEMIES. He reaches the INNERMOST CAVE where he endures the SUPREME ORDEAL. He SEIZES THE SWORD or the treasure and is pursued on the ROAD BACK to his world. He's RESURRECTED and transformed by his experience. He RETURNS to his ordinary world with a treasure, or ELIXIR to benefit his world.

Although that seems like a formula, it's not, and it shouldn't be treated as such. It's not a "cookie cutter" recipe but rather a map that frames the storytelling in a way that carries it forward and keeps the interest of the audience. The Hero's Journey approach can be found in many beloved films: 'The Dark Knight Rises', 'The Life of Pi', 'The Hobbit', 'Planes Trains and Automobiles', 'The Heat', 'The Godfather', all of which follow a rigorous structural approach to storytelling that builds on the audience expectations. They still surprise and transport us, but they follow narrative conventions that we all internalize as a result of living in a story-telling civilization.

People have natural expectations about how a story should evolve. They want to be moved emotionally and surprised without losing the thread of the story to the point where they start wondering: "Where is this going?" You want the filmmaker to innovate and lead audiences in a new direction but with enough guidance and comfort to keep that audience immersed in the story.

There are writing techniques and rules behind every story genre. Make sure the screenplay in front of you respects these rules. Sometimes it is okay to break these rules, under two conditions: you know the rules, and you know why you need to break them.

The Blake Snyder Beat Sheet

Others also use the "beat sheet" or the three-act structure as developed by the late Blake Snyder in the book *Save the Cat*. I personally believe that these two schools of thought are totally compatible. I strongly recommend reading Snyder's book because, among other things, it explains the 15 steps that are usually part of a great screenplay and even the approximate page where each step is situated.

Figure 2 Blake Snyder's Beat Sheet example

#	STEPS	DESCRIPTION	PAGE
1	Opening Image	Sets the tone, mood, type, and scope of the project. A "before" snapshot.	1
2	Theme Stated	Secondary character poses question or statement to main character that identifies the theme of the movie.	5
3	Set-up	Introduce or hint at every character in A story; plant character tics to be addressed later on.	1 - 10
4	Catalyst	Life-changing event that knocks down house of cards.	12
5	Debate	Point of no return; character makes a choice	12-25
6	Break into Act II	A strong, definite change of playing field. Do not ease into Act II.	25
7	B-Story	Often the "love" story; gives us a break from the tension of the A story; carries theme of movie; often uses new "funhouse" version of characters.	30
8	Fun & Games	"The promise of the premise" / the heart of the movie / all about having fun	30-55
9	Midpoint	Threshold between 1st half and 2nd half; can be false peak or false collapse; stakes are raised; clock is ticking, fun and games over	55
10	Bad Guys Close In	Bad guys regroup and send heavy artillery ; hero's team begins to unravel	55-75
11	All is Lost	Opposite (peak/collapse) from the midpoint / series of death - old way paradigm doesn't work /give up moment/escape attempts; false defeat; no hope	75
12	Dark Night of the Soul	Darkest point; main character has lost everything	75-85
13	Break into Act III	A story and B story combine to provide solution	85
14	Finale	Wrap-up; neutralize all bad guys in ascending order up to the most evil.	85-110
15	Final Image	Mirror of opening image; show change that has occurred	110

These "beats" (or steps) have also been consistently present in the best screenplays over the last century. The best-in-class financiers make sure that the story elements are in the right order to compel the audience to go to a movie theater and keep them engaged for two hours.

Movie audiences want to feel engaged, moved and entertained. Very few people go to the movies to be challenged. One Hollywood mogul once said to a producer: "If you want to send a message, go to Western Union." That is the blunt reality. It does not mean moviegoers cannot be challenged while watching a feature film, but the vast majority of filmgoers are not motivated to buy movie tickets by the prospect of being challenged. Challenging films by critically acclaimed filmmakers will continue to be made for reasons other than profitability, and we can only hope that public funding and philanthropists will continue to support these projects in the best interest of the advancement of cinema and our cultural identity. Investors in these films should be well aware that the lower commerciality of a project directly affects its revenue potential and its overall ability to break-even and eventually generate a profit. But sometimes the ROI is not only measured in dollars. It can be measured in social cause advancements, for example, or to bring light to an issue that needs to be made public.

Look for the five big "trailer moments"
Some film financiers will be looking for at least five strong scenes easily identifiable in a screenplay that can be become the backbone of the film's promotional reel called the "trailer". Trailers are shown to audiences in theaters before the feature presentation. They are usually assembled from the same distributor and often tailored to the same type of demographics or film genres. Shorter versions will be edited for TV and online advertising. A good mix of trailers is the most cost-efficient way to sell a film theatrically, because it speaks directly to a very valuable segment of the public: the film-going audience.

A variety of trailers will be developed to create a sustaining campaign; that simultaneously or successively target different audience segments, often based on a simple segmentation approach called the "four quadrants.". The four quadrants are respectively Men and Women under and over 25 years old. A distributor will often want to expand from a core quadrant into one or two more to reach critical mass and, consequently, will edit various trailers to please these different quadrants. More on the quadrants in Chapter 9...

Similar to an existing film, but with a new twist...

A familiar refrain in Hollywood is: "Give me the same thing, only different..." And while this might not make all that much sense at first glance, there is wisdom here as traditional audiences want something familiar on the one hand and yet fresh and innovative on the other.

Often, indie filmmakers are offended that film financiers and studio executives are looking for something recognizable or something similar to a film that has been a success. They ask me, why not a totally new story, a unique concept? It's a matter of risk. To sell a unique and "all-new-and-never-seen-before" concept, distributors have to risk significant amounts of marketing dollars with no guaranteed audience. They do it from time to time but they have to mitigate their risk like any business.

People choose their movies in a flash second

Since most moviegoers decide which film to watch quite spontaneously and often consult with at least another person, movies need to sell themselves very, very easily. Think about it: You came with friends to the multiplex and the big film you wanted to see is... sold out. Then you start to read the marquee screens, lookup your smart phones and exchange opinions about other films presented. Typically, someone will take the lead and try to sell the group another movie. In most cases, you will go for a film you can relate to, whether it's an actor, a sequel or a trailer you have seen before or that someone recommends. You will not spend hours to research the director and the cinematography behind the story.

That is why studios invest massive amounts of money on established franchises (ie. James Bond, Fast & Furious, Iron Man, etc.) and sequels of successful films. The trailer and the key cast also play significant roles in what movie ticket to buy.

The "cronut" syndrome

I like to compare commercial filmmaking to the food and hospitality business. We all like innovative gourmet chefs, and we celebrate their talent, but even they focus on starting from classics and giving them a new twist to make a new name for themselves. The recent introduction of the *cronut* in New-York City was a huge hit because people understood immediately that this was a cross between a French flaky croissant and an American fried donut. Bingo! The same goes for popular films.

Make the hero human: find the "save the cat" moment

Smart investors also know that the protagonist need to be sympathetic in some ways to the audience, otherwise they will not root for him or at least relate to him enough to keep interest in the story. That is why so many films include what we call a "*save the cat*[14]" moment early in the film, usually the first act, so that the audience can see the tender side to a hero that may be harsh or very aggressive, and that will make him more human and relatable.

The Blake Snyder categories

Some famous filmmakers have developed story categories that are now classics. According to Blake Snyder, there are ten categories that encapsulate most popular films based on audience expectations. See Figure 3 on the next page. These are also explained in more detail in his books "Save The Cat Goes To The Movies."

---

14 Save The Cat! The Last Book on Screenwriting You'll Ever Need, by Blake Snyder, Save the Cat! Goes to the Movies: The Screenwriter's Guide to Every Story Ever Told, by Blake Snyder.

Figure 3 Examples of films based on Save the Cat Categories

Categories	Themes / Films
Monster In the House A powerful creature intent on hurting the cast runs riot in an enclosed community. One of the cast is guilty of a 'sin' which facilitates the release of the beast.	Horror, house, sin (Alien, Fatal Attraction, Scream, The Ring, Saw, etc.)
Golden Fleece A hero must hit the road with his team of followers (or buddy whose skills and knowledge assist the hero) to obtain a prize or reach their goal.	Road movies. Team. Prize. (The Longest Yard, Planes, Trains And Automobiles, Saving Private Ryan, Ocean's Eleven, Maria Full of Grace)
Out Of The Bottle Magical, fantasy films. A hero who is granted a wish (desire). A spell is used as a framework to teach the hero a moral lesson.	Wish. Spell. Lesson. (Freaky Friday, Cocoon, The Nutty Professor, What women want, Groundhog Day.)
Dude/Dudes With A Problem. Action, drama, noir, thriller, sci fi, even horror and comedy, that deals with the ordinary guy brought into an extraordinary world, with a weakness to overcome in order to become a hero. Stakes are very high, usually life of death situations or mega catastrophes.	Innocent hero. Sudden event. Life or death Battle. (Three Days of the Condor, Die Hard, Sleeping with the Enemy, Deep Impact, Open Water)
Rites of Passage A hero reaching a crossroad such as adolescence, divorce, midlife crisis, retirement, parenthood. Usually the hero struggles to solve his problem. It gets worse before it gets better. The hero will evolve along the way, grow and accept his reality and make the best out of it.	Life problems, wrong way, acceptance. (Lost in Translation, Kramer vs. Kramer, Ordinary People, Trainspotting, Risky Business)
Buddy Love Stories based the need to be loved and accepted. Two people fight with each other but need still need to be together. A hero (incomplete) with a desire to fill a gap, whether it be physical, emotional, spiritual or practical. The	Incomplete hero. Counterpart. Complication. (The Black Stallion, Lethal Weapon, When Harry Met Sally, Titanic, Brokeback Mountain)

Categories	Themes / Films
counterpart is complementary to the hero but severe conflict exists that make the union almost impossible.	
Whydunnit	Detective. Secret. Dark turn.
Thrillers, crime, mystery, noir, gangster and detective films. An investigation that takes an unforeseen turn. Secret motives vary from money, sex, power, greed, fame etc. The detective makes a dark turn to solve the mystery.	(All the President's men, Blade Runner, Fargo, Mystic River, Chinatown)
Fool Triumphant	Fool. Establishment. Transmutation.
Comedy films. The fool is gentle and affable and bluffs his way through life. There is a "frenemy" or associate determined to see him fail. The fool must travel to an establishment or an unfamiliar, hostile, dangerous world in which he does not fit. Then transmutation happens.	(Being There, Tootsie, Forrest Gump, Legally Blonde, The 40-Year Old Virgin)
Institutionalized	Group. Choice. Sacrifice.
A group, a family, a corporation, a society or other oppressive system where the hero makes decides to take on the establishment to prove a point. A sacrifice is made and they must endure pain and hardship to prove their conviction and enrich their souls. The hero can rally, conquer or die.	(Platoon, The Godfather, One Flew over the Cuckoo's nest, Wall Street, Crash)
Superhero	Special Power. Nemesis. Curse.
A superhero with a special power usually used for the greater good to feed our need for morality. Often reluctant because they don't feel comfortable with saving the world. The hero has a nemesis, a rival, a bad guy can represent the ugly side of the superhero. He is as strong if not stronger than the superhero and knows his weakness and can curse him.	(Raging Bull, The Lion King, The Matrix, Gladiator, Spider-Man 2)

Although it can be seen as a series of clichés or a formula, it is fascinating to see how flexible and diversified the category system may be. I encourage you to read

Snyder's books, as you will discover how a proper tight structure is part of every good story.

The right packaging often starts with the director

A great story also requires the right talent (actors, actresses, director and key crew) to execute the story, connect with the audience and make the film a reality and a success. Often the choice of a great director will allow the project to attract the right actors.

Although a great story needs a great cast to reach the audience and be successful, the opposite is not true; the best cast will never compensate for a bad screenplay. The screenplay is the foundation on which you invest money, retain stars, actors, and directors to build a cinematic experience that people will want to see and positively text/tweet about when they leave a theater (or as we see more often during the film). That's what it's all about.

A good producer is able to tell you what his film is about in just a few sentences, and get you excited about it; if he's not, walk away. Film financing is already complex when you are indeed excited; it's a recipe for disaster when you feel bored by the story and/or the producer.

Request concise and precise info about the project

The savvy investor should require a summary of the project including the title, the genre and the logline (which is one or two sentences that will describe exactly what will happen to the protagonist and how he will get out of it.) The summary also includes a synopsis, one page usually, explaining how the various acts will unfold. Coverage (meaning a reader's report), and sometimes a treatment or an outline, are also key elements in choosing a project wisely, if you don't read the script yourself. I can understand that many financiers and investors simply don't have the time or interest in reading a 110-page screenplay. In that case, the investor needs to have an independent advisor who can read it and provide professional coverage on it.

Conclusion Chapter 7

- The film's screenplay and the basic story are the foundation of the project. It has to be great. It is the underlying property on which significant money will be invested. Smart investors are looking for a great story that deserves to be told.

- Sound narrative structure is crucial to entertaining and transporting audiences in fresh ways.

- The screenplay should contain scenes that make for great "trailer moments". At least 5.

- Avoid clichés and look for a new twist on a theme that people love.

- The hero has to be likeable or at least relatable

- Identify the film genre and how it is packaged.

- Make sure the project has a compelling logline and a good executive summary that captures the essence of the film.

- All rights should be cleared, with music rights being very important.

- The project should stand out as something many people would want to pay to see in a movie theater on a Friday night.

"Not everything that can be counted counts, and not everything that counts can be counted."

–Albert Einstein

Chapter 8
The Three Critical Pillars of a Successful Film Producer That Very Few Know

I can't emphasize enough that when an investor is looking for a project in film financing, he needs to assess the merits of the producer involved. This requires understanding the three pillars of a successful producer: <u>story</u>, <u>audience</u> and <u>profitability</u>[15].

1. Story

As we said in a previous chapter, the <u>story</u> is key, it's the foundation of the intellectual property in front of you, and it's the screenplay that will become the product on the screen. To come to fruition, it needs to be done by someone who has a passion for story, structure, plots, character arcs, set-ups and payoffs just to name a few - and who embraces the complexity of cinematic storytelling.

The key factors for narrative success are: a solid screenplay based on a story that deserves to be told, a director with a clear vision and a strong commitment to that screenplay – who, in turn, can attract the best talent given the limitations of the budget.

As an investor, you should have access to the proposed screenplay and professional coverage on it.

---

[15] For more insight on best practices for producers, I strongly recommend reading The Producer's Business Handbook by John. J. Lee & Anne Marie Gillen

2. Audience

The second element of focus should be audience. Whether we like it or not, we cannot strictly focus on the stories we like. We need to be convinced that there is a strong <u>audience</u> out there for that story. Whether it's a niche or very wide demographic, we still need to understand the size of the audience, where it is, what people in this group like, how the story compares to other stories that have been made into films and how they reached that same audience.

The key factors of success for the audience are: a good line-up of recent comparable films in terms of genre, budget and cast including their detailed revenue per window whenever possible.

From these comparables, the producer should establish a worst case and best-case scenario in terms of revenue.

3. Profitability

The third element is the <u>profitability</u> aspect of the project. What is the precise budget required to realistically make that story into a compelling film for that specific audience, so that expected revenues will materialize?

Key factors relating to success for profitability are: A sound budget, a rigorous pre-production, some cost control and risk mitigation measures, a balanced financial structure comprised of tax incentives, presales, debt and equity - as well as the ability to secure distribution and P&A funds for its release. Therefore a detailed budget made by a professional line producer and a detailed financial structure should be made available to investors.

This is a balancing act.

There is no "one size fits all" solution to any of these challenges, and as the project evolves, the producer's responsibility is to stay focused on these three elements. Therefore, as an investor, one of the simple questions that I like to ask the producers when they present the film project to us is "Why do you want to make this film?" "Why" is one of the most powerful questions you can ask. Depending on the answer, you'll gain a feeling as to whether the person understands the fundamentals of independent, commercially viable filmmaking.

Conclusion Chapter 8

Always keep in mind that the film needs to be based on a good story well told at a budget that makes the most financial sense in order to successfully reach a specific audience with a reasonable profit.

If you're able to answer these questions and tackle these issues with confidence, you will have so much more opportunity for distribution and be able to release the film successfully.

I'm a great believer in luck, and I find the harder I work the more I have of it.

–Thomas Jefferson

Chapter 9
The Importance of Distribution: Open on Friday...or Die

In the world of filmed entertainment, content is king, yes, but distribution is emperor. Unfortunately, the theatrical distribution distribution itself is highly unpredictable.

"Open on Friday or die". That means if you cannot bring in enough people in theaters for a Friday night opening, you're cooked. That is because with the proliferation of mobile devices and social media, a film that gets a cold review on a Friday evening has basically no chance of surviving the word of mouth or "word of fingers[16]." Social media can be a curse or blessing; it dramatically accelerates the buzz, good or bad, about a film or TV show.

Today the film distributor has to master a plethora of elements to be able to successfully open a film on a Friday night and compete with other distributors, as aggressive as they are, to get their share of the box office. From that opening weekend performance, distributors will be able to gauge the remaining revenue streams. That game requires a lot of capital and other resources. A lot is at stake. That is why without any P&A money, an independent film is poised to fail commercially.

Look at Figure 9 below. Here's an example of all the marketing initiatives that a big tent pole franchise will put in place to successfully build an audience for a film opening. The marketing team behind the release will build awareness

---

[16] The expression "word of fingers" is the digital equivalent of word of mouth. People use their mobile apps and their social platforms to review films as soon as they leave the movie theater.

and compete with the other film and entertainment choices available at the time - to open the film using free publicity, advertising platforms, social media and sneak previews. Independent films may tap into the same types of initiative albeit on a much smaller scale.

Figure 9 Typical Marketing Initiatives for Big Studio Releases

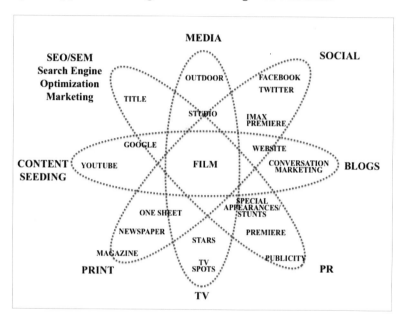

Distribution is where the profit is

In the commercial chain of value of a motion picture, distributors are in a very interesting position, as they retain a 25 to 30 percent fee from the theatrical rentals. However, the majors are currently struggling with a couple of challenges:

- VOD and SVOD revenues have not offset the decline in DVD sales yet.

- Studios face rising costs for production and marketing that cannot be easily passed on to consumers, as movie ticket prices remain mostly flat.

- Studio revenue increase stems from international markets - such as China - where the exhibitors are allowed to keep a bigger share of the box office.

Studios produce fewer films

As we saw in Table 5 in Chapter 3, the studio output of new films produced internally has decreased significantly in the last decade. Many studios end up distributing more independent films to keep their relative distribution clout and market share with theater exhibitors and to absorb their fixed costs.

Studios are distributors

Studios are always looking for new revenue sources in the form of fees charged to third parties to alleviate their fixed costs. Consequently, an investor in an independent film should always scrutinize the studio distribution agreement for hidden fees and various costs calculations because it may significantly impact the net revenue available and profit participations.

For instance, there could be "hold back" provisions in the agreement in favor of a domestic distributor. A hold back provision is a contractual right given to a distributor to delay the distribution of the film for a period of time. This is justified by the fact that distributors will try to find the best timing to release the film theatrically, but it should always be limited. In a perfect world, a hold back shouldn't exceed three months, but we've seen cases where such a provision dragged on for 15 months.

What's the impact of this? Well, if you are waiting for revenues from international markets, you may hear from your foreign buyers that, until the film is released in the United States, they will not be able to market it in their territory. So, in reality, you may have a domino effect by delaying the domestic release of the film, which negatively affects your international sales revenue collection. If you are an investor lending money against these international revenues, the holdback provision in the domestic agreement has an impact on you, and you should understand it.

Film success measures: marketability and playability

The distributor will assess the intrinsic value of the film before he agrees to take it on, based on its potential marketability and playability. The marketability measures the film's appeal to <u>potential</u> viewers, and the playability measures how <u>actual</u> viewers receive it.

Certain companies[17] that specialize in script evaluation will assess the marketability and playability of screenplays. Films are tested with approximately 1,500 moviegoers at a price per test of approximately $5,000.

Typically the distributor separates the audience of a film into four quadrants as you can see in Figure 5 on the following page: very simply, women and men above and below 25 years old. The studios will be looking at films that resonate with two or more quadrants (ideally all four quadrants), and they will build on the film elements that speak more to each quadrant.

---

[17] One of those companies is called OTX Media CT owned by IPSOS research.

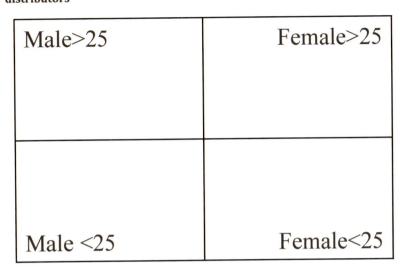

For example, an action film like *"Act of Valor,"* with real active-duty soldiers on a mission to bring back a hostage safely, could identify specific themes based on the four quadrants as per Figure 6 below.

Figure 6. Hypothetical Four quadrants matrix for *Act of Valor*

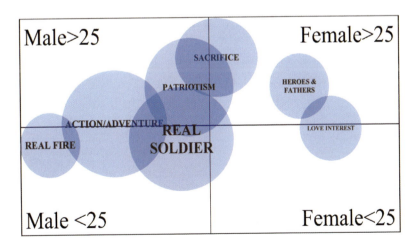

In this case, the film primarily resonates with a male audience. But the distributor would in all likelihood also tap into how women respond to the underlying themes of love, patriotism and family. After all, movie going often involves more than one person; attracting viewers in more than one quadrant is crucial to reach critical mass.

The various types of theatrical release

There are four types of releases for independent films. The differences lie in the number of screens and theaters that will be secured for showing the film. Accordingly, the P&A budget will have to include adequate print fees and media buys.

1. A **wide release** is generally between 600-4,000 screens.
2. A limited release/**platform release** is below 600 screens and often starts with 20-30 screens.
3. An **art-house release,** more limited, is aimed at a niche "repertoire" audience in specific markets.
4. A **"four wall" release** requires a filmmaker/producer to rent a screen in a movie theater and pay the staff the theater overhead in exchange for keeping all the box office revenues.

When to release a commercial independent film in theaters

Releasing an independent film is very tricky. You want to tap into a period where people are available but you don't want to compete head to head with huge studios blockbusters that will drain all the media attention and audience awareness.

Some of the best times for releasing an independent film are during the winter - the second and third weeks in January, all of February and March, up to spring break. May, June and July are earmarked for blockbusters.

While you may have a chance in mid-August, September and October are definitely great months to release indie films. Be aware that October to December is another studio blockbuster season, and you may struggle to garner your share of awareness.

Some independent distributors will still get traction for their films during the Oscar season buzz which helps maintain awareness. Harvey Weinstein of The Weinstein Company has mastered this release strategy, and his Oscar lobbying efforts often bring additional revenue to the company's films prior to and after the Oscar telecast.

The four major film markets
Berlin, Cannes, Toronto and Santa Monica are the four major annual film markets. Buyers from each territory have the opportunity to screen footage, and peruse scripts and budgets in order to make commitments. Banks or private lenders may then collateralize the presales contracts signed at markets in order to finance a portion of the production cost.

Sales and presales from primary and secondary territories
The most robust international territories are often termed "primary" as their value is easier to finance with banks. They include UK, France, Germany, Russia, China, South Korea, and Australia. The value of territories such as Greece, as well as Spain and Italy to a certain extent, have been under intense scrutiny is recent years due to their economic difficulties and national solvency issues.

The secondary territories may be a little riskier or offer lower revenues. Keep in mind that when you review a film project, you should always assess the unsold territories very conservatively and look at what is referred to as "ask and takes" from your producer's sales agent.

The asks vs. the takes
The "ask" is the price that the sales agent intends to request for a given territory, and the "take" is the minimum amount that he's willing to accept, his floor price. But

sometimes agents may be too optimistic and end up getting less than their floor price.

If you loaned money against those unsold territories, and sales agents end up selling them for much less than planned, you may have a problem recouping you loan and your premium. As a lender, it's good business to validate these international sales estimates with another sales agent and an experienced senior lender to have a more informed opinion. Once estimates are adjusted to the investor's assessment, a discount should be applied on those revenue figures to be more conservative.

Table 13 on the next page illustrates the average value of minimum pre-licensing fees (i.e. presales) that a good sales agent can expect for a film given its budget size. (*This table is only for example purposes as the ongoing rate varies constantly.*)

Table 13 Example of minimum pre licensing fees from international territories per budget size

Average Minimums	Budget sizes (in Million USD)			
	0.75-1	1-3	3-6	6-12
Territory	*Typical Minimums (in thousands of dollars)*			
WESTERN EUROPE				
Benelux	$20-40	$40-80	80-125	125-250
France	$40-80k	$80-160k	$160-400k	$400-850k
Germany/Austria/ Switz.	$50-100k	$100-300k	$300-600k	$600-1.2m
Greece	$5-10k	$10-30	$30-50k	$50-90k
Israel	$5-10	$10-15	$20-40	$25-50
Italy	$50-100	$100-250	$250-550	$550k-1m
Portugal	$10-20	10-20	20-40	80-150
Scandinavia	$50-100	100-225	225-350	350-700
Spain	$40-80	80-150	150-400	400k-1m
Turkey	$15-35	35-60	60-125	125-175
United Kingdom	$40-80	80-200	200-500	500k-1m
EASTERN EUROPE				
Czech Republic / Slovakia	$10-20k	20-50k	50-75k	75-175k
Former Yugoslavia	$5-10k	10-15k	15-25k	25-50k
Hungary	$10-30k	30-60k	60-100k	100-200k
Poland	$10-30k	30-75k	75-125k	125-200k
Russia	$30-60k	60-175k	175-350k	350-600k
ASIA PACIFIC RIM /OCEANIA				
Australia/New Zealand	$25-40k	$40-75k	$75-125k	$125-225k
China	$5-20k	$20-40k	$40-75k	$75-150k
Hong Kong	$5-15k	$15-25k	$25-75k	$75-125k
India	$10-20k	$20-40k	$40-60k	$60-125k
Indonesia	$10-15k	$15-30k	$30-50k	$50-100k
Japan	$50-100k	$100-300k	$300-600k	$600k-1m
Malaysia	$5-10k	$10-25k	$25-75k	$75-125k
Middle East	$5-10k	$10-20k	$20-40k	$40-90k
Pakistan	$2-5k	$5-10k	$10-20k	$20-30k
Philippines	$5-10k	$10-35k	$35-75k	$75-125k
Singapore	$10-15k	$15-30k	$30-75k	$75-125k
South Korea	$30-80k	$80-275k	$275-500k	$500-950k
Taiwan	$10-40k	$40-100k	$100-200k	$200-350k
Thailand				
LATIN AMERICA				
Argentina/Uruguay/Paraguay	$10-20k	$20-40k	$40-75k	$75-120k
Bolivia/Ecuador/Peru	$5-10k	$10-20k	$20-40k	$40-60k
Brazil	$20-50k	$50-100k	$100-200k	$200-400k
Chile	$5-15k	$15-25k	$25-40k	$40-75k
Colombia	$5-10k	$10-20k	$20-35k	$35-75k
Mexico	$15-50k	$50-100k	$100-225k	$225-450k
Venezuela	$5-10k	$10-20k	$20-40k	$40-75k
AFRICA				
South Africa	$10-15k	$15-30k	$30-50k	$50-90k

Always use sales estimates with caution. They are one of the most frequently amplified documents presented in the financials of a film project.

The myth of finding distribution at Sundance

It cannot be emphasized enough that obtaining distribution is a real challenge. Sometimes producers assume that they have a serious chance of getting their film presented at Sundance Film Festival and are overly confident it will trigger a distribution agreement.

Consider these figures: In 2013, Sundance received 4,044 feature film submissions, of which only 113 were selected. Only 33 films were acquired for distribution, of which a mere 15 were paid a minimum guarantee of a million dollars or more. While the highest reported payment was $9.75M, most of the films acquired were around the million-dollar mark. Selling an independent film for ten million dollars at Sundance is a very rare exception indeed.

Keeping domestic distribution as a potential upside

If the producer has been successful in closing the financing of the film without having to sell all domestic rights, there may an upside for the equity investor. For that upside to materialize, however, the finished film needs to be strong enough to be picked by a distributor for theatrical release. In addition, box office revenues will initially cover the exhibitors share, the distribution fee, the P&A loan and other payees before the remaining sums flow back to the producer and its equity investor.

Many filmmakers now hope that such burgeoning platforms as Home Media – including video-on-demand (VOD) such as Cable-on-demand, Vudu and iTunes, as well as subscription-video-on-demand (SVOD) services like Netflix, Hulu and Amazon – will provide much needed recoupment money. But although these digital services increase in popularity, they keep the detailed usage data very confidential, making it quite difficult for indie producers to forecast revenues.

The Netflix phenomenon

Netflix has quickly become a dominant distribution player, with more than 40 million subscribers worldwide as of early 2014. Its streaming subscription service provides ease of access and depth of choice for what is perceived as a reasonable amount per month.

What makes Netflix even more interesting is its ability to track its users' behavior. They know what you watch and when you watch it; also they know when you stopped watching during a film, and are able to identify viewing patterns very precisely. The same goes for other streaming and VOD services.

But even if they have access to a gold mine of data, I believe there will always a sizable part of unpredictable factors regarding what may appeal to viewers in moving forward. You cannot predict with absolute certainty what trends may pop up or what audiences will be raving about down the road.

That is why audacious artists and smart business people keep an open mind about what people may want to experience that they don't even know about.

Pressure on costs for acquisitions and original content

A couple of years ago, Netflix was in urgent need of content and signed generous multi-year agreements with studios such as Disney. These agreements will start to kick in gradually and may squeeze Netflix's operating margins. But while films are an important component of their library, they do not build Netflix's brand as fast as original programming. Their biggest competitor, HBO, understood that early on and developed live boxing events and original series such as *The Sopranos*, *Six Feet Under* and, more recently, *Game of Thrones* with significant success. In the same vein, Netflix has now targeted more money towards original series such as *House of Cards* and *Orange is the New Black* to become a premium-viewing destination offering "must-see" programming.

It's very possible that Netflix's studio deals, its direct investment in homegrown TV series and its increasing Internet bandwidth costs may reduce the license fees paid for acquiring independent films. The more dominant a platform becomes, the more pressure it's able to apply on small suppliers. Nevertheless, Netflix is still a place where many independent films can find an audience.

Conclusion Chapter 9

- Distribution, a costly undertaking, is an essential step of the exploitation of a feature film. Without distribution, to put it bluntly, there is no revenue.

- When a film is released in theaters, it has only one chance to make a first good impression. Open on Friday or die.

- A film marketing campaign will tap into traditional media, social media, publicity (free media), content seeding and Internet search optimization. The number of screens made available will dictate the amount of capital required to open the film.

- Distribution is the most profitable sector of the filmed entertainment industry.

- Distributors have significant capital costs and overhead to absorb and they will pass these costs onto your project whether you like it or not.

- It is the investor's responsibility to understand all the applicable fees featured in the various agreements - and to make sure they are negotiated fairly.

- It is generally easier to release an indie film when the studios are not opening their big blockbusters. You may get more attention.

- All presales are not created equally, depending on the territory, the international distributor involved and the sales agent assigned to the project.

- Very few films presented in festivals secure distribution.
- Domestic distribution is difficult to obtain. However it also helps international sales to have a domestic distribution signed.
- Netflix and all streaming services are game-changers for distribution. Licenses paid for independent films will continue to be under pressure.

I'm only rich because I know when I'm wrong...I basically have survived by recognizing my mistakes.

−George Soros

Chapter 10
How Smart Investors Find and Negotiate the Best Projects: Teamwork!

No magic!

You know by now that there is no secret recipe or magical formula for success in film entertainment, nor is there a guarantee of profitability. Whether it's Netflix data mining or the now infamous so-called Monte Carlo[18] model algorithm developed by Ryan Kavanaugh's Relativity Media, no one really knows for certain the precise box-office of an emerging project. That being said, investors that do their homework, work hard, operate in a collaborative fashion and know how to ask key questions have a significant edge against the competition.

The team

As we mentioned before, a serious investor will put his funds into escrow quickly and take the time to negotiate the best deal afterwards - before the close of financing.

Two types of professionals can often be enlisted to support savvy financiers. Independent business advisors should be utilized to assess the creative value of a project, review the sales estimates provided by the producer and negotiate and properly structure the debt or equity investment. And an experienced entertainment lawyer aligned solely with the investor's interests can help make

---

18 At Relativity, Ryan Kavanaugh developed a model based on a Monte Carlo algorithm designed to predict the chances of success of a motion picture. To this day, however, not all of their releases have reached stellar box-office performance.

sure all agreements properly reflect what has been negotiated.

Many contractual definitions to review

Contracts are critical because all agreement definitions and accounting practices are uniquely defined and determined for each film - and often for each participant. In other words, terms such as gross receipts or net profits have no intrinsic meaning; the definition will be specific to each agreement, which is one of the reasons to get expert advice along the way before you sign any contract.

If the investor considers a film that is part of a multiple slate, he needs to understand how the cross-collateralization in other films will affect his participation in a specific film. How will a loss on a film project affect the other film's recoupment? That is a complex issue that requires due diligence.

Investors are in the business of obtaining the best return at the lowest cost possible. But while they certainly should not spend inordinate amounts of money on advisors, they also should never leave important questions unanswered. Investors should fully understand the magnitude of the risks presented. When you're in doubt, always ask for clarification. If you don't ask the proper questions, don't expect other parties to proactively provide the answers for you. As a colleague once said, "if you don't know who has the losing hand around the table when the financing closes, it's probably you."

You reduce your own risks and improve your chances of making a favorable return by negotiating a series of conditions with the producer and the completion guarantor - and by understanding and negotiating your priority position within the recoupment structure.

There is no better question to ask a producer than "*Show me in the agreement who gets the money in what order specifically. Walk me through the waterfall recoupment so I fully understand it.*" That question may raise eyebrows, but you need to get an educated answer to determine if the contractual elements reflect what is being pitched to you.

I strongly believe that, at the end of the day, the financier himself is the only person to make his business decisions about film investments. If he relies only on lawyers to make that decision, he is disengaging from the investment process. In my view, lawyers should be concentrating on the legal forms and the protection of the legal interests of the client, but the negotiation of the business points and deal terms themselves should involve the client with or without a separate advisor.

Chapter 10 Conclusion

- There are no magic recipes for a successful film investment.
- Film financing structures are somewhat complex by nature and often require a small team to work collaboratively; a creative expert, a lawyer, a sale agents and a film financing advisor should help the investor make an informed decision on how to approach the opportunity.
- A good negotiator and a rigorous albeit flexible approach make a big difference.

"Don't tell me what you value, show me your budget, and I'll tell you what you value."

–Joe Biden

Chapter 11
Trust but Verify... The Real Due Diligence Process!

When former US President Ronald Reagan discovered the Russian proverb "Trust but verify"[19] back in the 1980s, he thought it was so compelling that he had it engraved on a desk plate in the Oval Office. This phrase became his mantra and he used it frequently when discussing U.S. relations with the Soviet Union and their lengthy negotiations on nuclear disarmament.

As a financier of a film project, you have to trust the capabilities of the people with who you're working to make a successful movie. If you don't trust them, don't even consider investing. But if you do trust them, that doesn't mean you have to be blind. While a source of information might be considered reliable, an investor should always do his due diligence to verify that such information is accurate and trustworthy.

Sometimes the producer makes representations in good faith, but the due diligence may reveal inaccuracies even unknown to him.

Remember that when in doubt always ask questions. Answers given to questions - such as the ones below - can be very useful:

- Why do you want to make this film?
- How exactly do you expect this film to generate revenues at each window of exhibition?
- What is it based on?

---

19 The original Russian proverb is a short rhyme, which states *"doveryai, no proveryai."*

- How do the profits flow back?
- In what order is the money coming back?
- How do you get paid in this transaction?
- If you add up all your various fees, how much are you getting compensated?
- Are there other places where you or your company will obtain a fee from this transaction directly or indirectly?
- Do you get rebates from vendors and, if so, where are these rebates reflected?
- Is there a cap on these expenses and, if not, why not?
- Is there a completion bond in place?
- What are the three biggest risks in this project?
- Is there a hold back provision on the domestic distribution agreement that could impact the international sales delivery and collection?
- Is there a minimal interest charge paid to the lender?
- Are you giving the investor a legal expense allowance?
- Is the interest compounded monthly or annually?
- How exactly is the waterfall recoupment working? Can you walk me through it?
- Given your timeline to recoup my investment, what is the net ROI that I can expect?
- What is the producer's experience and track record in that specific genre and budget size?
- How are the director and key cast perceived and valued commercially in both domestic and international territories?
- Are the actor contracts "pay or play" or "pay and play"?

- Where is the chain of title?
- Who created this budget? Is he or she a unit production manager (UPM) or a line producer? What are the credentials?
- Is the recoupment *pro rata* or *pari passu*?
- What percentage of the international presales and tax credits is the senior lender financing against?
- Have you looked at all state tax incentive programs before deciding where to shoot the film?
- What about postproduction incentives?
- What is your view regarding contingencies?
- How does the producer get his money?
- How does the distributor get his money?
- Is the interest rate based on LIBOR[20]?
- Are the talent contracts conditional on obtaining a completion bond and a review of the chain of title?
- How does the bond company calculate its fee? On what budget items?
- Why should I accept a boiler plate deal if it doesn't apply or make sense in this case?
- And so on…

If you feel you may not fully understand how the answers impact your investment, retain the services of people that have a complimentary expertise to your own. Only when you are fully satisfied in writing with all the conditions preceding your disbursement should you proceed with your investment.

---

[20] London Inter Bank Offered Rate

The investment should be typically made at the closing of financing, once a completion bond is in place[21]. Then the real work begins. Once your money is disbursed, there's still the need to copiously track the project. Most people think that, at that point, the work is done - and you just sit back and wait for repayment. However, as a financier, you should track weekly cost reports to make sure that all expenses are appropriately allocated and that no hidden fees or no unnecessary charges are levied. More specifically, you should keep in mind that the contingency should only be spent if absolutely necessary. Therefore, that 10 percent contingency already built into the budget can help offset unforeseen bad news down the road.

A typical due diligence process can have as many as four phases. Here is a detailed explanation of each phase.

1. DUE DILIGENCE PHASE
When a prospective investor is presented with a film financing opportunity, he should negotiate a definitive escrow agreement with the production borrower.

- The investor will deposit the amount agreed upon by the parties into an escrow account with a mutually approved financial institution subject negotiating and coordinating execution of a definitive escrow agreement.
- The escrow agreement will expressly provide that all terms and conditions of a term sheet will require complete satisfaction before the investor's funds are released from the escrow account; including but not limited to: finalization of long form documentation between the parties, closing of the senior financing indebtedness, and issuance of a completion guarantee drawn in favor of the investor.
  - The release conditions included in the agreement will

---

[21] In the case of bridge financing, the completion bond is never in place. Therefore, the higher risk commands a higher return. Also some very low budget films may not have a bond. Always use extreme caution before investing in a project that has no completion guarantee.

permit a financial expert and legal counsel, acting on behalf of the investor, to comprehensively conduct all customary due diligence, and review and evaluate all corroborating documentation relating to the entire financing transaction, including but not limited to:

- o Chain of title documentation
- o Financing plan
- o Senior loan documentation (intercreditor & inter-party agreements)
- o Key cast & crew contracts
- o Completion guarantor agreement
- o Bonded production budget
- o Sales agency agreement
- o International & domestic licensing agreements
- o Collection management agreement
- o Priority recoupment of preferred equity or subordinated debt

- In the event that, by a certain date specified in the escrow agreement, a term sheet is not agreed upon by the parties or fully executed or the film financing transaction has not close, the escrow holder is contractually instructed to refund the amount on deposit in the escrow account to the investor.

2. ESCROW DISBURSEMENT PHASE

After the investor's funds are deposited into the escrow account, they are to be released to the completion guarantor - for scheduled disbursement to the production borrower - upon final closing of all financing expressly in accordance with the long form loan documentation agreed upon by the parties.

3. PRODUCTION PHASE

Throughout the entire production of the film, a financial advisor should actively act on behalf of the investor to review and evaluate weekly cost reports and analyze budget variances to ensure strict adherence to the production schedule and the related production budget.

4. COLLECTION PHASE

Upon full repayment to the senior debt lender, revenues from commercial exploitation of the film are to be collected and administered by a mutually agreed upon third party collection agency. The collection agent will periodically account to and systematically distribute all monies received strictly in accordance with a pre-negotiated collection agreement. The investor's advisor should closely monitor that all exploitation revenues from domestic and international are received promptly by the collection agent and remitted to the investor throughout the collection phase.

Conclusion Chapter 11

- The due diligence phase of an investment in film or television should never be overlooked.
- It is crucial for determining the real risk and mitigating some of the unknown risks.
- Ask questions and make sure the answers are satisfactory and reflect the various agreements.

How many millionaires do you know who have become wealthy by investing in savings accounts? I rest my case.

–Robert G. Allen

Chapter 12
How to Mitigate the Most Insidious Risks and Find Hidden Savings

All investments by nature contain elements of risk, and film financing is no different. You create a brand new project every time, and there's no guarantee of public enthusiasm and willingness to buy the product in its various platforms. and by forces of market usually present a risk adjusted return.

The goal of this book is to help investors identify and overcome as many of the potential risks as possible and gauge the proper adjusted return for that risk. But that's only half the work. Once the return is determined and agreed upon, it's the job of the investor and his advisor to mitigate these risks and track them as closely as possible to create a distinct competitive advantage to the investor.

There are different risks;

- First and foremost, the risk of not completing the film. For this reason, it is indispensable to have a bond in place before the investment is made. It will guarantee that the film will be completed on time and on budget.
- International buyers could delay or turn down the film - if they have a problem with the finished product - jeopardizing payments. It has happened before, it could happen again. Having reputable partners in the project can help alleviate that risk; a big bank, a serious sales agent and a Collection

Account Management (CAM) agency have more leverage to get paid that a sole investor.

- There's also the risk of injury, death or the inability to utilize or proceed with a key cast of a film. You should be able to get essential elements insurance so that, if something were to happen, the investment is insured.

- Don't overlook the risk of intellectual property infringement, which should be covered by Errors & Omissions insurance. The insurer will require a legal opinion about the chain of title.

- There's a risk of bad debt on receivables. To offset that risk, the advisor to the investor should to provide due diligence on the reputation of international and domestic sales agents and distributors involved. Another option is to insure receivables, although that will cost the investor some additional money. The insurance company will only kick-in after all other recourses to get paid have been exhausted.

- Another risk concerns the film's negative, which could be seized by the lab for unpaid invoices. For that matter, always insist on obtaining a lab pledge holder agreement and a lab access letter.

- A further risk relates to sales expected from certain territories not materializing: that's why the initial assessment of these unsold territories and their systematic discounting is important.

- There's a risk that the film goes over budget - but because you should have already negotiated a completion guarantee, the bond company will be assuming that risk for you. In very rare instances, the bond company could call the bond and interrupt or impose to finish the film because it is responsible for the overspending.

- There is always the clichéd risk that a producer, God forbids, could abscond with your money. If you have a completion bond in place, your funds will normally go to the bank or the completion bond company, and they will disburse the fund to the producer, as the production schedule necessitates.

- One may also face the risk of a distribution company forwarding revenues. Typically, when there are many parties involved in the financing, there's an interparty collection agreement and a third party agency chosen to alleviate that risk.

- A disappointing theatrical release is obviously another risk. If you are not comfortable betting on the performance of the film, you can prefer projects where you lend money against international sales. As an equity investor you cannot expect to have a guarantee of performance.

- Like in any businesses, there's always the inherent risk of having to sue to exercise your contractual rights. Taking legal action is a last resort and it's always costly. It's more desirable to negotiate all the possible outcomes within the agreements prior to disbursing the funds.

- And finally, there's a genuine risk of being taken for a ride in terms of recouping your investment. This is the very reason why you need to negotiate by writing your waterfall priority from the outset.

Areas to find possible savings

Experienced investors will be looking in hidden corners of the budget for possible economies:

- One of the line items is called "acquisition of rights." As an investor, you should always pay attention to that budget section to make sure that costs have not been inflated by selling or transferring rights to a series of loan-out companies.

- Another section you must scrutinize carefully is the completion bond fee. The percentage paid to the completion guarantor should exclude any costs that they would not likely spend if and when they have to take over a production.

- Financiers should also focus on interest charges: are they compounded monthly or annually? Depending of the circumstances, the variance may be substantial.

- Locations that offer tax advantages can play a huge part in a film financing structure without sacrificing the creative elements.

- If you are involved in a project that is struggling to get the financing completed, ask yourself the following questions to help reduce the budget:
  o Have you considered deferments for some of the vendors or participants?
  o Have you considered actors working for scale and a percentage of the back end?
    o Have you thought of reducing the distributor fee to a more acceptable level?
  o How can you finance your tax credits?

Other worthwhile questions include:

- How can you reduce the holdback provision in the domestic deal?
- How can you avoid future litigations?
- How can you spread your risk across more than one project without investing blindly in a slate or investing in less interesting projects?
- How can you avoid huge expenses in development?

It is argued that an investor should always get comfortable with the worst-case scenario and have in mind a *pre-mortem*[22] as opposed to a painful *post-mortem*. In other

---

[22] A pre-mortem is to imagine that a project has failed, and then work backward to determine what could possibly lead to the failure. It's a preventive measure to identify what can derail the project and address it proactively.

words, hope for the best but prepare for the worst. Having a conservative approach improves your chances of meeting and surpassing your objective.

Conclusion Chapter 12

- The savings you can extract and the contractual arrangements you negotiate before closing can make a big difference in your ROI.
- Do your homework, ask questions and insist on clear answers.

Frugality includes all the other virtues.

–

Cicero

Chapter 12.5
How to Track Revenues and Costs
To Get Your ROI

Once you've completed your due diligence and you're satisfied that the investment meets your criteria, you proceed with the disbursement of funds through an escrow agreement. Then the heavy lifting starts. If you spend the energy and resources tracking costs and revenues of the project as it evolves, you increase your chances of being successful. Your advisor should be looking after your financial interests by analyzing weekly variances to budget during principal photography and postproduction - where all the big spending occurs.

Keep an eye on the reserve for contingencies

Although it's often assumed that the 10% contingency reserve is totally spent by the end of postproduction, this is not always the case. As the name implies, this reserve is a "cushion" for major and unforeseen circumstances that cannot be absorbed in the current schedule and budget. If not spent, it should flow back to refund the first payee, i.e., the senior lender.

Sometimes, savings created during production and unspent contingencies are very helpful in accelerating the repayment of senior debt, thus expediting the recoupment of other stakeholders down the line.

A 20 million dollar production budget includes a customary 10%, (2 million) contingency. It is a significant reserve, and can make quite a difference in terms of profit or loss for an investor.

- Keep a close eye on actual costs, and remember that the contingency is only used if absolutely necessary.
- Don't hesitate to give the producer and the director financial incentives for staying on budget without resorting to the contingency.
- Request in your agreement that any budgetary savings or unspent contingency will automatically accelerate the repayment of the senior lender. By doing so, you just increase your chances of recoupment.

Ask for the weekly cost reports

You or your advisor should review costs on a weekly basis and flag any concern to the producer or the bond company.

The shorter the recoupment period, the better

There's usually more than one window to recoup a film investment, but the most important windows for recoupment are theatrical, video on demand, and home media. The longer you wait to recoup your investment, the smaller your net return on investment will become. Time is money, and as Harold Vogel[23] said in his book, "... even with the assistance of important marketing and distribution platforms such as YouTube and Facebook, it is still remarkably difficult to monetize the new found accessibility and interest in niche products".

Conclusion Chapter 12.5

- It's your money: ask for reports and make sure your capital is spent wisely and according to plan.

---

[23] Source: *Entertainment Industry Economics, Harold L. Vogel p. 50.*

- If you are successful, you may very much want to re-invest in a film project, perhaps with the same filmmakers.

- A bulletproof process will only improve things for everybody in the long run.

- After all, as a smart investor, you are looking for a transparent investment with a favorable risk-adjusted return where you feel your capital is safeguarded as much as possible.

- It if you follow the appropriate steps, this is indeed possible.

The only place where success comes before work is in the dictionary.

–Vidal Sassoon

Conclusion

The independent film industry presents its own unique opportunities and challenges for investors

As we've seen in this book, making a successful film is a fascinating and complex process:

- A team of handpicked talented artists and professionals must work as a team to bring a great story to the screen for a pre-determined audience.

- The various phases of execution are all crucial in maintaining the proper balance between production costs and the potential audience in order to generate a reasonable profit for its investors.

- A good film produced at the right price with a very specific & measurable audience in mind has much more of a chance to secure distribution.

Fascinating and unpredictable

As much as we use refined tools to try to predict audience tastes and build on past successes of film franchises and best-selling books, there are no performance guarantees for any movies. In fact, the element of surprise in each new film makes it exciting for the consumer.

One should also keep in mind that entertainment options have multiplied in recent years – not only at the multiplex but at home and on various mobile screens. As a financier, the film you're about to invest in needs to have the ability to touch people enough so that they want to spend money to see it.

A risk many investors are willing to take

However, every year a number of independent films break through to become box office marvels and provide generous returns to their investors – provided that up-front agreements have been properly negotiated. Table 14 below illustrates recent examples of films with limited budgets compared to studio movies - that took in colossal amounts of money from theatrical and home entertainment revenues.

Table 14. Examples of recent low budget films generating gigantic theatrical revenues
Source: www.the-numbers.com

Release Date	Title	Production Cost	Gross Sales[24]	Cost to sales ratio
Sep-09	Paranormal Activity	$450,000	$216,124,813	0.21%
Jan-12	The Devil Inside	$1,000,000	$105,486,721	0.95%
Apr-11	Insidious	$1,500,000	$112,334,078	1.34%
Oct-10	Paranormal Activity 2	$3,000,000	$197,629,331	1.52%
May-12	Chernobyl Diaries	$1,000,000	$43,950,077	2.28%
Aug-10	The Last Exorcism	$1,800,000	$78,943,335	2.28%
Sep-13	Insidious Chapter 2	$5,000,000	$172,329,135	2.90%
Jun-13	The Purge	$3,000,000	$101,279,188	2.96%
Nov-10	The King's Speech	$15,000,000	$471,135,101	3.18%
Oct-12	Paranormal Activity 4	$5,000,000	$154,083,195	3.25%
Nov-08	Slumdog Millionaire	$14,000,000	$419,603,886	3.34%
Jun-12	Magic Mike	$7,000,000	$207,827,849	3.37%
Dec-10	Black Swan	$13,000,000	$359,649,855	3.61%
Jun-09	The Hangover	$35,000,000	$712,495,312	4.91%

When you compare the gross sales of these films with their production costs, you can understand why so many people are able to afford a beach house in Malibu. I cannot think of many other businesses where you can generate more than 200 million dollars with an initial cost of 450,000 dollars. Because most of the financial risk is front-loaded, your marginal cost is very limited. If you hit a home run,

---

[24] Gross sales include Worldwide Gross Box Office receipts and Home Video Gross Revenues.

such as those listed above, your back-end profit participation will be very favorable.

What is your reason for investing in films?

As an investor reading this book, you may already have an interest, a passion, for this industry. You may also simply want to diversify your portfolio from bond & equity market pressures. And some may even want to support a talented friend or family member who has a story to tell, a film to shoot or a company to start. Whatever the reason, using common sense is always advisable.

Our industry will always attract financiers looking for "status investments" because they provide unique perks and benefits in addition to potential financial returns. As much of a thrill as it may be to walk the red carpet with Halle Berry or see your producer credit on the big screen, don't be swayed by all the glamour and stick to your investment principles.

In summary, the film business in general, and independent production in particular, present a number of compelling investment opportunities. And if you follow the simple rules of this book – the "little secrets" that elite investors keep hush-hush – you, too, maybe become an elite investor. And who knows… we may see you at your movie on a Friday… and laughing all the way to the bank on a Monday!

END

GLOSSARY

Above the line Costs: term denoting portion of a film's budget, usually including the writer, director, producer, and main cast.

Access letter: a letter under which a laboratory undertakes to honor orders placed by a distributor, even though the laboratory may be owed money by the producer or, in relation to the film, by other persons.

Adjusted gross deal: a distribution agreement where the distributor deducts from gross receipts the costs of promotional advertising and divides the remaining balance, the adjusted gross, with the producer. The advantage for the producer is that he does not have to directly provide or incur the distribution expenses. The disadvantage is that the distributor may cut back on distribution expenses, to the detriment of the commercial success of the film, if he does not think his share of adjusted gross receipts will cover his expenses.

Ancillary rights: rights that may be capable of commercial exploitation that accrue or are acquired as a result of or in the course of production of a film, as distinct from the exploitation of the film itself. They include merchandising rights, television spin-off rights, sequel, prequel, and remake, book publishing rights, computer game rights, soundtrack album rights and the music publishing rights in the score. These rights are sometimes referred to as secondary rights.

Answer print: the composition print that emerges from the laboratory after the combination of the sound with the graded picture, optical effects and soundtrack. When the print is approved a computer tape is made which tells the printer what to duplicate and ensures that all subsequent copies are the same. Also known at the first trial print.

Assignment of security: the method by which a financier takes a security interest in a film. The copyright in the film and the underlying rights (and the revenues) are assigned to the financier by way of security. Effectively they are mortgaged to the financier to secure the repayment of the financier's investment.

Below the line costs: term denoting portion of a film's budget excluding all elements that are considered above the line.

Cap: an arrangement between the provider and the borrower where, for a premium, an upper limit is set on the interest rate payable by the borrower on a floating rate loan. If the underlying interest rate rises above the upper limit, the provider of the cap reimburses the borrower for the excess above that limit.

Cash flow: in the film production jargon, cash flow often refers to the financial drawdown schedule required to pay for the cost of physically producing a film.

Certification: the cost of production of a film, as certified by an independent firm of accountants.

Chain of title: the route by which the producer's right to use copyright material may be traced from the author to the producer through a "chain" of assignments and transfers.

Co-operative advertising: Advertising, the cost of which is shared between the distributor and exhibitors.

Co-production: a film produced through the co-operation of, and with substantial contributions from, two or more production companies.

Co-production treaty: an agreement between nations that may permit films made in or with resources from both nations to benefit from subsidies available from both.

Collection agreement: an agreement entered into by the producer and financiers of a film with a collection agent. The collection agent is appointed to collect the proceeds from the exploitation of the film and distribute them to the financiers, the producer and other beneficiaries, such as deferees and profit participants, in accordance with directions set out in the agreement. The collection agent would expect to receive a fee for this work, perhaps negotiated as a percentage of all sums collected by it. A collection agent is appointed because, while a production entity may have a continuing legal existence, it may not have a continuing physical existence in the sense of numbers of individuals who attend to its business on a daily basis. The collection agent offers physical continuity and is responsible for ensuring that distributors account for and pay the producer's share of the distribution revenues. The collection agent will hold revenues in trust and they are therefore intended to be secure from the collection agent's own creditors. The collection agent may also offer a degree of security, not only in the legal sense, but also because of its professional reputation and perceived permanence.

Completion guarantee: an agreement under which a completion guarantor guarantees to the financiers of a film, or a distributor who has advanced money prior to delivery, that the film will be completed and delivered by a given date to its principal distributors in accordance with the relevant distribution agreements.

Completion guarantor: a company that is in the business of providing completion guarantees for financiers.

Contingency: a final sum added to the budget for a film to cover unforeseen circumstances, usually 10% of the budgeted costs excluding the completion guarantee fee.

Copyright search: a search in the US Copyright Office to see if any interest in the relevant work or film has been registered.

Cost of funds: a bank's cost of lending money. This will depend on the nature of the loan – for example a bank's cost of funds on a sterling LIBOR loan will usually be LIBOR plus.

Costs off the top deal: a distribution agreement where distribution expenses are deducted from gross receipts and the balance is then divided between the distributor and the producer in agreed shares. Distributors' fees are usually calculated on gross receipts but in this case the distributor's share is effectively its fee, calculated on a lower base.

Cross collateralization: the application of revenues derived from one source, whether a territory or a means of exploitation, towards the recoupment of an advance irrespective of revenues arising from another territory or means of exploitation all falling within the same grant to a distributor or agent. This device is generally discouraged by the lawyers of independent filmmakers, but is widely encouraged by sales agents as a means of facilitating sales.

Deferee: a person to whom a deferment is payable.

Deferment: a sum payable to a writer, performer, director, producer, or someone else connected with a film out of revenues derived from the exploitation of the film, but typically after the deduction of distribution fees and expenses and, usually, after the financiers and the completion guarantor have recovered all of the sums they have advanced towards the cost of production and delivery of the film.

Deficit: difference between the required budget of film and the amount of finance already raised. Also known as Gap.

Discount: to discount, for example, a distribution agreement means the assignment to a lender of the benefit of a distribution agreement under which advances are payable on delivery of the film in return for a loan, which can be used to meet the costs of production of the film as they are incurred. The agreement is "discounted" because the sum made available by way of loan is less than the amount of the advance. The difference covers the lender's fees and legal expenses and the interest calculated to be payable on the loan during the period under the contracted repayment date.

Discounted Cash Flow or DCF: an investment appraisal technique that takes account of the time value of money by assessing the present value of future income and expenditure. It is often used in valuing intellectual property or to show the viability of a project.

Distribution agreement: an agreement under which rights to exploit a film in one or more categories of media are granted. The distributor grants rights as principal, not as agent. The agreement will provide either for a lump sum payment by the distributor or for a sharing of revenues.

Distributor: A film distributor is a company or individual responsible for releasing films to the public theatrically.

Domestic DVD/ Blu-ray Gross: The total dollar income to the studio from units shipped to rental and retail in the first 3 months of release.

Domestic DVD/ Blu-ray Units: The raw amount of total units shipped, before losses, in the initial run or first 3 months of shipments to retailers in the United States and Canada.

Domestic Free TV Revenues: The revenue earned from licensing fees paid by multi-channel providers, derived from advertiser-supported television of any kind, be it distributed by network or syndicated broadcast in the United States and Canada.

Domestic Gross: Total amount of revenue generated by a film at the box office during its theatrical run in the United States and Canada

Domestic Pay TV Revenue: The revenue earned from licensing fees paid by multi-channel providers, derived from non advertiser-supported television, whether through cable, satellite, or pay per view in the United States and Canada. *This number does not include revenue from ancillaries i.e. digital downloads, VOD, or web streaming.

Domestic Print Advert Cost: The estimated cost of film prints supplied to exhibitors (theatres) and the advertising/marketing costs involved in the initial release of the feature film.

Domestic Rentals: The Distributor's share of the domestic gross revenues on a film, which is typically 40-50% of the gross revenue in the United States and Canada.

Domestic rights: the rights to distribute a film in North America. The world excluding North America is, just as confusingly for a non-American, often collectively referred to as "foreign."

Domestic VHS Gross: The raw currency amount retailers totaled from consumer purchases of VHS units, before losses, in the initial run/first cycle of shipments to retailers in the United States and Canada.

Domestic VHS Units: The number of physical units shipped to retail stores for sale in the United States and Canada.

DVD/ Blu-ray Release Date: The disc was available in stores for purchase by consumers on this date.

Equity of redemption: the borrower's right to redeem (i.e., cancel) a mortgage on payment of the sums secured.

Errors and Omissions (E&O) insurance: insurance against claims arising out of infringements of copyright, defamation and unauthorized use of names, trade names, trademarks or characters. The producer of a film usually takes out this insurance if the film is intended to be distributed in North America on a film-by-film basis. This type of insurance will typically commence from the first day of principal photography or from delivery. Coverage will be forfeited if the claim arises out of an active failure to act that is "willful, wanton, intentional, malicious or conspiratorial" or if the production procedures laid down in the policy are not adhered to. The principal insured may be asked to have the financiers and distributors named as additional insureds.

Favored nation (or Most Favored Nation, MFN): the most favorable terms accorded to a party in a transaction, including that no- one will get any better terms or if any improved terms are granted to a third party then the "favored nation" will be treated equally.

Feature film: a film with a running time of over 72 minutes made with the intention of securing a theatrical release.

Film Title: The name of the film used in theatrical distribution and exhibition.

Final cut: the final say on the editing of a film. This right will usually lie with the production company (subject to its obligations to financiers and distributors), unless the director is of sufficient stature to be able to insist on this right as a term of his agreement with the production company.

Financial covenants: the undertakings within loan documents requiring the borrower to maintain certain financial ratios, for example, current assets to current liabilities, or total debt to total equity, or to maintain a minimum net worth during the term of the loan. Such covenants would not be applicable where the business of the borrower consists only of the production of a single film.

Floating rate: interest at a rate that fluctuates, typically by a reference to changes in the Prime Rate or LIBOR or the base lending rate of a specified bank.

Foreign rights: the converse of domestic rights, which are the rights to distribute a film outside North America.

Four walling: the practice where a producer rents all the seats or all the shows for a week (usually at a discount) and then puts in his/her own film and collects the box office.

Free television: a television broadcast intended for reception by the public where no charge is made to the viewer.

Fringes: social security and, in some cases, pension, health, and welfare payments due to the cast and crew on top of wages shown in the below the line section of the budget. Fringes are often detailed in a separate schedule and summarized in a line in the final section of the budget top sheet.

Gap: difference between the required budget of the film and the amount of financing already raised.

Gap financing: a specialty lending arrangement whereby a bank will lend the difference between production finance raised and the minimum expected from sales by a reputable sales agent.

Genre: The genres/categories (one per film) are as follows: action, adaptation, animation, biopic, comedy, crime, documentary, drama, erotic, family, fantasy, foreign, horror, musical, mystery, performance, period, political, remake, rock 'n' roll, romance, sci-fi, sports, thriller, war, western.

Gross participation: an arrangement under which a participant in a film, usually a major artist, will share in gross receipts, rather than net, receipts.

Grossing-up clause: a clause customarily found in loan documents which provides that, where withholding taxes are imposed on payments by the borrower to the lender, the borrower will pay an additional amount to the lender so that the lender receives what it would have received had there been no such taxes. The additional payment is referred to as a "gross-up payment" and the requirement to pay as a requirement to "gross up".

Hedge: in a financing context, any technique to offset the impact of movements in interest rates or currency exchange rates. Typical examples of hedging instruments are swaps, options and forward rate agreements.

Holdback: a period during which a particular form of exploitation is not allowed. A video gram hold back, for example, means a period following theatrical release that must expire before video grams of the film can be released.

Hollywood Studios: certain US-based companies that own physical locations and facilities for film development, pre-production, production, and post-production. They also have subsidiaries responsible for film production, distribution, and in some cases, exhibition. The most well known of these are Columbia/Tristar (Sony), Universal, MGM, Paramount, 20th Century Fox, Walt Disney, and Warner Bros.

Increased costs clause: customarily found in loan documents, this clause provides that if there is a change in regulatory requirements that raises the cost to the bank of making or maintaining a loan (or reduces its effective return) after the loan agreement is signed, the borrower will compensate the lender.

Independent film: a film made without the direct financial participation of the Hollywood Studios.

International Free TV Revenues: The revenue earned from licensing fees paid by multi-channel providers, derived from advertiser-supported television of any kind, be it distributed by network or syndicated broadcast in foreign countries.

International Gross: Total amount of revenue generated by a film at the box office during its foreign theatrical run.

International Home Video Revenue: The distributors foreign gross revenues generated from (wholesale) international DVD, Blue-ray, VHS video sales.

International Pay TV Revenue: The revenue earned from licensing fees paid by multi-channel providers, derived from non advertiser-supported television, whether through cable, satellite, or pay per view in foreign countries. *This number does not include revenue from ancillaries i.e. digital downloads, VOD or web streaming

International Rentals: The Distributor's share of the domestic gross revenues on a film, which is typically 40-50%

of the foreign gross revenue.

Internegative: when a film has been shot on color reversal stock, a duplicate stage (interpositive) is omitted by making a CRI (color reversal internegative) from the camera negative. An internegative is made directly from this to produce a duplicate negative from which exhibition print copies of the film are made.

Interparty Agreement: the interparty agreement regulates the relationship between various financing parties to a film.

Interpositive: a positive print, made from the original negative of the final version of the film, from which a duplicate negative is made. It is then possible to make exhibition print copies from the "dupe" negative without damaging the original negative. Also known as the master positive.

Laboratory letter: an expression used indiscriminately to refer to access letters and to pledge holder agreements, without differentiating between the two. While the functions of an access letter and a pledgeholder agreement may be fulfilled in a single document, the respective functions are distinct.

Lead bank, or lead manager: a bank that acts as lead manager for a potential syndicate of banks in relation to a syndicated loan. Appointed by the borrower, the lead manager, in exchange for a fee, normally settles with the borrower the outline of the basic terms of the loan, promotes the loan to potential participants, provides information relating to the borrower and its business and negotiates on behalf of the participants. Lead managers try to ensure that they are not obliged to provide the loan if insufficient participants express an interest, that they are not liable for the information provided to participants and that they are not liable for any act or omission when negotiating the loan.

Letter of Credit (LC): a written undertaking to pay the sum

155

of money, on delivery to the person giving the undertaking, of documents in the form specified in the letter of credit. When a distribution agreement is discounted, the lender may insist that the advance payable by the distributor is secured by a letter of credit from a recognized bank. The documents required to trigger payments usually include a certificate from a third party, which is often the completion guarantor, that delivery has been made to the distributor in accordance with the distribution agreement. Once an independent producer has convinced a financier to participate, the financier can then provide a LC upon which the producer can borrow. The costs of preparing the LC are usually borne by the producer.

LIBOR: the London Interbank Offered Rate, being the rate at which a bank is able to borrow money on the London interbank market from lending banks. LIBOR varies according to the size of the borrowing and its period.

Limited partnership: a partnership constituted by a general partner (with unlimited liability) and limited partners (with limited liability). Limited partnership is a form of association frequently used to enable investors to invest collectively. Normally, the general partner will manage the investment.

Limited recourse: a loan similar to a non-recourse loan but where there is some recourse to the assets of the borrower other than those charged, and sometimes limited recourse to other companies. The latter may take the form of a limited parent company guarantee.

Loan out agreement: an agreement where the services of an individual are made available through a production company, usually owned or controlled by that individual.

Loss payee endorsement: confirmation from a completion guarantor's reinsurer, given to a film's financiers, to the effect that they can look directly to the reinsurer to make payments under the reinsurance policy in the event that the completion guarantor has a liability to make payment under the completion guarantee.

M&E Track: a mixed music and effects track that is free from dialogue. Used for foreign language versions.

Margin: in a banking context, the rate of interest payable to a lender over and above LIBOR or the lender's base rate – for example 2% over LIBOR.

Max Screens: maximum number, at any given time, of theatres the film was played in exhibition.

Minimum guarantee: the minimum sum a distributor guarantees will be payable to a producer as a result of the distributor's distribution of the film. The guaranteed sum may be payable at the beginning of the distribution period, as an advance against the producer's share of the proceeds of distribution. It may, however, be the aggregate sum that the distributor guarantees will be payable to the producer over the whole of the distribution period. Any shortfall of actual revenues against the guaranteed amount would then be payable at the end of the distribution period.

MPAA: the Motion Picture Association of America administers the rating system for feature films in the USA in a manner not unlike that in which the BBFC does in the UK.

MPAA Rating: The Motion Picture Association of America's film-rating system, used in the U.S. and its territories to rate a film's thematic and content suitability for certain audiences. Ratings include: G, PG, PG-13, R, and NC-17.

Negative Costs: The estimated cost of physical production (below & above-the-line-costs involved in completing a film and producing a negative). *Negative cost excludes distribution fees, overhead, interest, and profit participation. *Negative cost includes only the minimum guaranteed fees to actors and other talent and excludes residuals.

Negative pick-up: a distribution agreement where the advance is payable only on delivery of the finished film to the distributor.

Negative pledge: a covenant contained in loan documents where the borrower agrees not to create or permit to exist any other mortgage, charge or security interest over any of its assets.

Net present value or NPV: today's value of money to be received or paid in the future after applying a discount to reflect the delay before it is received or paid. The accuracy of the result depends on the assumptions made in assessing the discount rate.

Non-recourse loan: a misnomer for a loan where the lender has no recourse to any party or any assets other than the assets over which the lender has specifically taken security, in effect the proceeds of exploitation of the film, and/or the single purpose vehicle which owns the assets.

Novation: the transfer of all benefits and obligations under a contract. The transfer requires the consent of the person to whom the obligations are owed. This is to be contrasted with an assignment, which is the transfer of the benefit only of a contract or other right, and may not require the consent of the person owing the obligation.

Non-theatrical rights: the rights to exhibit a film to a live audience by direct projection by means of sub-standard gauges (for example 16 mm or 8 mm) or by video, where the exhibition of films on a regular basis is not the primary purpose and when no specific admission charge is made for the exhibition. The exercise of non-theatrical rights is usually limited to educational establishments, nursing homes, hospitals "shut in locations" – such as prisons, convents and orphanages – and clubs and other organizations of a religious, educational, cultural, charitable, or social nature.

Off-balance sheet finance: an arrangement under which a

loan is made to a company without the debt appearing on the investor's balance sheet.

Optical sound negative: to make optical-sound combined prints, the final master magnetic mix is re- recorded as a photographic optical sound negative. This negative is synchronized and printed with the final cut picture negative on positive stock, to make the married print.

Option: in the context of film, an option is a right exercisable during a specific period for a specific sum to acquire certain rights, for example the right to produce a film based on a book.

Output deal: agreement between a film producer and distributor – or between a film producer and a television company – under which the distributor or television company obtains in advance the distribution or television rights to a number of films to be made or distributed over a period of time.

Overages: distribution revenues payable to the producer after the advance or minimum guarantee has been recouped.

Overspend: where the actual cost of production exceeds the budget.

P&A: Printing and Advertising. The cost of promoting a film. Paying for the film to be put into cinemas and for advertising it in all media.

Packaging: the provision, usually by a talent agency, of a package of individuals to work on a film. The package may include the director, screenplay writer, stars and members of the supporting cast. The package is usually presented as a whole in that you cannot choose only some elements.

Panning and scanning: the process by which a film shot on an aspect ratio (the ratio of the width to the height of the picture) suitable for cinema distribution (e.g., 1.85:1 or 2.3:1) is reduced and adjusted for television transmission (standard screen 1.33:1, widescreen 1.8:1). When a film is shot for both theatrical distribution and television transmission the viewfinder is often "masked" to ensure that the main action is within the television aspect ratio.

Pay or play: a commitment to pay a director or performer made before production commences, and sometimes before all the finance has become unconditional, regardless of whether his or her services are used.

Pay television: television for which viewers pay a subscription. Normally received directly from satellites or via cable.

Pick-up: a film for which the distribution rights are acquired after it has been made.

Pledge holder agreement: an agreement under which a processing laboratory agrees with the financiers of a film not to part with possession of the original negative and the principal film material without prior written consent of the financiers.

Points: shares of back end or net profits in a film are measured in percentage points. To have points in a film means to have a share of the net profits.

Pre-sale: a license or distribution agreement entered into before a film has been completed. The advance, minimum guarantee, or license fee payable under the pre-sale may form part of the finance package for the film, either as a direct contribution towards the cost of production or, if the advance, minimum guarantee or license fee is only payable on or after delivery of the film, it may be discounted.

Priority agreement: an agreement between the guilds, financiers and, sometimes, the completion guarantor, regulating the priority of their respective security interests in the film.

Private investor: an individual, often having little direct connection with the film industry, who invests his/her own money in a film.

Producer's share of net profits: net profits are what is left of revenues from the exploitation of the film after distribution fees and expenses, repayment of any loans and investments raised to finance production, repayment of any sums extended by the completion guarantor and the payment of any deferments. Net profits are normally divided between the investors and the producer. The producer's share is usually between 40% and 60% of the net profits, out of which the producer may have to pay the profit entitlements (points) of various individuals and others who have contributed towards the film. These shares are fixed either as a share of the producer's share of net profits or as a share of 100% of the net profits.

Release Date: The date on which a completed film is legally authorized by its owner for public distribution and theatre exhibition.

Residual: a sum of money, payable under a union, guild or individual agreement, to a performer, musician, writer, composer, director or producer by reference to the means by which, or the place in which, the film is exploited.

Revolver or revolving facility: a loan facility that requires loans to be repaid at the end of given periods, which enables the loans to be immediately redrawn at the end of those periods subject to a final repayment and termination date.

Sale and leaseback: a sale of an asset that is immediately leased back to the seller by the buyer.

Sales agent: an agent appointed by the producer to act as agent for the sale of the film.

Security agreement: a charge or mortgage of the copyright and distribution rights in a film and of the physical materials created in the process of producing the film given by the production company as security for the repayment of a loan or investment used to finance the cost of production of the film.

Single purpose vehicle or SPV: a company established for a particular project or to hold a particular asset. The borrower's group often uses an SPV to contain insolvency risk.

Source material: the original work on which the screenplay for a film is inspired by or based upon.

Stop date: the last date on which a performer or director can be obliged to work. A performer or director may want the certainty of knowing when he/she will be free to accept another engagement. Stop dates are unpopular with completion guarantors, as it can be very expensive to replace an important member of the cast or the director if a film is delayed under a bonded agreement.

Subordinated debt: debt, the repayment of which is postponed or subordinated to more senior debt.

Syndicated loan: a loan provided by a number of banks (called a "syndicate") as opposed to a "bilateral loan" between one lender and the borrower.

Takeover: completion guarantors and some financiers require a right to take over the production of a film if the producer becomes insolvent, commits a material breach of its obligations to the completion guarantor or the financier encounters serious production problems. This may involve firing some of the crew and/or cast working on the film, including the director.

Tax haven: a jurisdiction that charges no tax or tax at very low rates. Examples are the Channel Islands, Isle of Man, British Virgin Islands, Netherlands Antilles, Bermuda and Cayman Islands.

Television rights: the collective expression includes a number of different forms of television, such as free and pay television and terrestrial and satellite television. When granting television rights, care should be taken to be specific as to the rights granted if revenues are to be maximized.

Theatrical rights: the right to exhibit the film in cinemas and other places of public viewing to which the general public is admitted and for which an admission charge in money or money's worth is made.

Title search: a report, usually carried out by agents in the USA, on registration of works under the proposed title of the film and on literary works, television programmers and films bearing the same or similar titles to that proposed for the film. The report may include a digest of references to projects bearing the same or a similar title that have appeared in the film industry trade press.

Total Net Revenue: Total Gross (Domestic/International Theatrical Gross + VHS/DVD/Blu-ray Gross + Domestic/International TV Revenue) – Negative Cost – P&A Spend

Turnaround: when a project is developed, the person financing the development has an agreed period in which to put the project into production, failing which the projects goes into turnaround. When this happens the producer generally is entitled to acquire the project back from the financier, usually for all or a proportion of the sums advanced by the financier.

Underspend: the amount by which the budgeted cost of the film exceeds the actual cost of production of the film.

VHS Release Date: The VHS unit was available in stores for purchase by consumers on this date.

Week One Rank: The box office rank the film debuted in theaters, one week after the release date.

Weeks In Release: The number of weeks a film played in theatres.

Window: the period for which a film is available for viewing in any particular medium.

About The Author

Rene Bourdages is a veteran entertainment executive with more than 30 years of senior level operating experience. Mr. Bourdages held many high level executive positions before focusing his managerial skills on entertainment media consulting in Canada and Los Angeles.

Prior to founding Elevado Media, he was President of CBC (Canadian Broadcasting Corporation) merchandising from 2004 through 2011. He has also held Executive Vice President positions at Quebecor/Groupe TVA and Astral Media Movie Premium TV channels with direct responsibility for up to 1,200 employees and gross revenues of nearly $200 million. Previously, Mr. Bourdages served as Director of the Harold Greenberg Fund, which finances the development and production of Canadian feature films.He holds a Certificate in Business and Management of Entertainment from UCLA.

He is a Chartered Board Director, Laval University Governance Program and was selected as one of Canada's Top 40 under 40.Mr. Bourdages is a member of the Academy of Television Arts & Sciences and the American Film Institute.

ELEVADO MEDIA provides executive consultancy services in the entertainment industry relating to financing, distribution and marketing of feature films, television and transmedia.Our clients consist of high net worth individuals, wealth management and family offices as well as producers and distributors looking for specific solutions to their growth strategy.

Visit www.e;evadomedia.com, or reach out to Rene on LinkedIn or via email at rene.bourdages@elevadomedia.com.

Made in the USA
Charleston, SC
16 November 2016